PRESIDENT'S MALARIA INITIATIVE

Senegal

Malaria Operational Plan FY 2016

TABLE OF CONTENTS

ABBREVIATIONS and ACRONYMS

ACT	Artemisinin-based combination therapy
ANC	Antenatal care
BCC	Behavior change communication
CBO	Community based organization
CDC	Centers for Disease Control and Prevention
cDHS	Continuous Demographic and Health Survey
CFA	West African Financial Community Franc (USD $1 = F CFA 500)
CHW	Community health worker
CMS	Central Medical Stores
DHS	Demographic and Health Survey
DSDOM	*Dispensateur de soins à domicile* (village malaria worker)
FY	Fiscal year
GHI	Global Health Initiative
Global Fund	Global Fund to Fight AIDS, Tuberculosis and Malaria
HIV/AIDS	Human immunodeficiency virus /acquired immunodeficiency syndrome
IDB	Islamic Development Bank
IEC	Information, education, communication
IPTp	Intermittent preventive treatment for pregnant women
IRD	*Institut de Recherche pour le Développement*
IRS	Indoor residual spraying
ITN	Insecticide-treated bed net
JICA	Japan International Cooperation Agency
LLIN	Long-lasting insecticide-treated bed net
LNCM	*Laboratoire national de contrôle des médicaments* (National Drug Control Laboratory)
M&E	Monitoring and evaluation
MIP	Malaria in pregnancy
MIS	Malaria indicator survey
MoH	Ministry of Health
MOP	Malaria Operational Plan
NMCP	National Malaria Control Program
PBF	Performance-Based Financing
PECADOM	*Prise en charge à domicile* (home-based management of malaria)
PMI	President's Malaria Initiative
RDT	Rapid diagnostic test
SMC	Seasonal malaria chemoprevention
SNEIPS	National Health Education and Information Service
SP	Sulfadoxine-pyrimethamine
SP-AQ	Sulfadoxine-pyrimethamine/amodiaquine
UCAD	*Université Cheikh Anta Diop*
UNICEF	United Nations Children's Fund
USAID	United States Agency for International Development
USG	United States Government
WHO	World Health Organization

I. EXECUTIVE SUMMARY

When it was launched in 2005, the goal of the President's Malaria Initiative (PMI) was to reduce malaria-related mortality by 50% across 15 high-burden countries in sub-Saharan Africa through a rapid scale-up of four proven and highly effective malaria prevention and treatment measures: insecticide-treated mosquito nets (ITNs); indoor residual spraying (IRS); accurate diagnosis and prompt treatment with artemisinin-based combination therapies (ACTs); and intermittent preventive treatment for pregnant women (IPTp). With the passage of the Tom Lantos and Henry J. Hyde Global Leadership against HIV/AIDS, Tuberculosis, and Malaria Act in 2008, PMI developed a U.S. Government Malaria Strategy for 2009–2014. This strategy included a long-term vision for malaria control in which sustained high coverage with malaria prevention and treatment interventions would progressively lead to malaria-free zones in Africa, with the ultimate goal of worldwide malaria eradication by 2040-2050. Consistent with this strategy and the increase in annual appropriations supporting PMI, four new sub-Saharan African countries and one regional program in the Greater Mekong Subregion of Southeast Asia were added in 2011. The contributions of PMI, together with those of other partners, have led to dramatic improvements in the coverage of malaria control interventions in PMI-supported countries, and all 15 original countries have documented substantial declines in all-cause mortality rates among children less than five years of age.

In 2015, PMI launched the next six-year strategy, setting forth a bold and ambitious goal and objectives. The PMI Strategy 2015-2020 takes into account the progress over the past decade and the new challenges that have arisen. Malaria prevention and control remains a major U.S. foreign assistance objective and PMI's Strategy fully aligns with the U.S. Government's vision of ending preventable child and maternal deaths and ending extreme poverty. It is also in line with the goals articulated in the RBM Partnership's second generation global malaria action plan, *Action and Investment to defeat Malaria (AIM) 2016-2030: for a Malaria-Free World* and WHO's updated *Global Technical Strategy: 2016-2030*. Under the PMI Strategy 2015-2020, the U.S. Government's goal is to work with PMI-supported countries and partners to further reduce malaria deaths and substantially decrease malaria morbidity, towards the long-term goal of elimination.

Senegal was selected as a PMI country in FY 2007. This FY 2016 Malaria Operational Plan presents a detailed implementation plan for Senegal, based on the strategies of PMI and the National Malaria Control Program (NMCP). It was developed in consultation with the NMCP and with the participation of national and international partners involved in malaria prevention and control in the country. The activities that PMI is proposing to support fit in well with the National Malaria Control strategy and plan and build on investments made by PMI and other partners to improve and expand malaria-related services, including the Global Fund to Fight AIDS, Tuberculosis, and Malaria (Global Fund) malaria grants. This document briefly reviews the current status of malaria control policies and interventions in Senegal, describes progress to date, identifies challenges and unmet needs to achieving the targets of the NMCP and PMI, and provides a description of activities that are planned with FY 2016 funding.

The proposed FY 2016 PMI budget for Senegal is $22 million. PMI will support the following intervention areas with these funds:

Insecticide-treated nets (ITNs): During FY 2015, PMI supported the distribution of free and subsidized long-lasting insecticide-treated bed nets (LLINs) nationwide via multiple continuous distribution channels. These include free LLINs to pregnant women attending antenatal care (ANC) clinics and to primary school children, subsidized nets to other health facility clients through community-based organizations, and through social marketing. To promote demand for and correct use of LLINs, PMI has also invested in behavior change communication (BCC) activities using primarily community-based networks. With FY 2016 funding, PMI and the NMCP plan to continue supporting the routine distribution system to bridge the gap for those who do not possess an LLIN and to replace worn out nets. PMI plans to procure 1.2 million LLINs to support routine distribution. The total LLIN need for 2017 is estimated at 2.2 million.

Indoor residual spraying (IRS): During FY 2015, PMI supported targeted IRS activities in four districts sprayed in previous years. Pyrimiphos-methyl was the insecticide of choice for this year because of the insufficient longevity of bendiocarb. Nevertheless, sufficient supplies of bendiocarb remained from the previous stock to cover one district. In two of the districts where pyrimiphos-methyl was used, spray operations began in May 2015. In the other two districts, although the pyrimiphos methyl was used in one, spray operations began in July to maximize the effective duration of the bendiocarb and to reduce operating costs. A total of 111,201 structures were sprayed (97% of those targeted) and 434,201 people were protected. With FY 2016 funds, PMI will support the NMCP's plan to spray malaria hot spots in selected districts based on incidence and entomological data. Eligible areas include districts and/or health post zones with an incidence greater than 50 per 1,000 in the previous year and with indoor resting and biting malaria vectors.

Malaria in pregnancy (MIP): The NMCP adopted intermittent preventive therapy for pregnant women in 2003 and the strategy is implemented in all ANC sites nationwide. National policy has recently been revised to include World Health Organization (WHO) recommendations on frequency (at least three doses starting in the second trimester and with at least one month between doses). The NMCP recommends using quinine to treat pregnant women with confirmed malaria in the first trimester and ACTs in the second and third trimesters. During FY 2015, the Government of Senegal continued to procure SP for IPTp while PMI focused its support on training and supervision of health workers in malaria in pregnancy activities. With PMI's assistance, registers have been updated to reflect all three doses of IPTp and these are now being used in health facilities nationwide. The NMCP monitors the proportion of women who receive three doses of IPTp among those who attend at last one ANC visit, a proportion that increased from 14% to 35% in the last year. PMI's FY 2016 funding will continue to support activities aimed at reinforcing the provision of effective MIP services in health facilities. Support will continue for monitoring and supportive supervision of MIP service delivery, improvement of data collection including IPTp data, and training of new staff on IPTp, including topics such as the importance of LLIN use in pregnancy, diagnosis and management of MIP, and counseling and interpersonal communication skills.

Case management: The NMCP adopted ACTs as first-line treatment in 2006 and introduced RDTs in 2007. In addition, pre-referral treatment with rectal artesunate for severe malaria and seasonal malaria chemoprevention (SMC) are WHO recommendations already adopted by Senegal's NMCP. At the community level, PMI supports both health huts and home-based management of malaria (PECADOM), as a means to reach as many people as possible with proper malaria case management. With FY 2016 resources, PMI plans to support training and supervision for microscopic diagnosis of malaria, quality control for microscopy and RDTs, and procurement of microscopy consumables and RDTs. The number of RDTs required is expected to remain high as the malaria testing algorithm expands in Senegal and more active case detection activities are carried out in the context of pre-elimination. PMI also plans to procure ACTs, injectable artesunate, and antimalarials needed for SMC in the high-transmission regions of Senegal. In addition, PMI plans to support malaria training and supervision both in the formal health sector and at the community level. Finally, PMI plans to support the implementation of single low-dose primaquine for transmission reduction in elimination districts and also antimalarial efficacy monitoring.

Health systems strengthening and capacity building: During the past year, PMI's health systems strengthening activities included continued support to the Central Medical Stores, support for institutional capacity building at the NMCP, and support for ongoing results-based financing activities. Integrated logistics supervision visits were conducted at all regional medical stores and health districts, and PMI also supported the NMCP to supervise case management at hospitals, health centers, and health posts. With FY 2016 funding, PMI plans to support activities to develop capacity at sub-national and central levels to continue working towards the attainment of the NMCP's pre-elimination objective. PMI will complement other Mission health programs to promote local governance by strengthening the capacity of local elected officials to address malaria as a priority in local development plans and increasing participation of communities in decision-making and financing. Also, PMI will encourage the NMCP to empower their staff at the decentralized level to plan, manage, and coordinate activities and allocate resources as appropriate to achieve expected results.

Behavior change communication (BCC): The NMCP's Strategic Framework for 2014-2018 emphasizes that IEC/BCC approaches in Senegal should be evidence-based and tailored to specific populations and geographic areas. PMI has supported various community mobilization and BCC activities in Senegal. These include both ongoing malaria communications (mass and interpersonal) and communication activities promoting specific events, such as IRS or LLIN distribution campaigns. Typical communications activities in Senegal have included community meetings on a specific topic, home visits, theater, community radio, and social mobilization. With FY 2016 funds, PMI will continue to support a range of communications activities to influence the social and behavior changes needed to improve the adoption of key malaria prevention and care seeking behaviors (e.g., net ownership, proper net use, net repair, IPTp, when and where to seek care). PMI will also continue to support communication activities to accompany IRS and SMC campaigns.

Monitoring and evaluation (M&E): The second round of the continuous DHS (cDHS) was completed in 2014-2015 showing sustained levels of intervention coverage from the 2012-2013 cDHS results. During the past 12 months, PMI continued to support 20 epidemic surveillance sites with the expansion to more health posts and districts to support expanding reactive case detection activities. Using FY 2016 funds, PMI plans to continue support for the expansion of case investigation in northern districts, contributing to key data collection and analysis activities. PMI will also continue to support data collection through the cDHS to monitor intervention coverage. FY 2016 support from PMI will also support process monitoring for SMC in Senegal and the development of an M&E course for the NMCP.

Operational research (OR): The NMCP's research agenda has a two-pronged approach: developing and evaluating tools to eliminate malaria in low transmission districts, while developing and evaluating tools to decrease transmission toward pre-elimination levels in the higher transmission southern districts. PMI has funded four operational research studies, all of which fit under this rubric, namely: a study on burden of malaria among nomadic pastoralists and access to interventions supported efforts in the north, and studies on the diagnostic algorithm, acceptability of SMC, and factors affecting ongoing high transmission in districts in which all interventions had been scaled up. PMI will support operational research to add molecular diagnostics to samples collected from children under five during the continuous DHS, to determine the proportion of sub-microscopic asymptomatic parasite reservoir depending on transmission zone and to examine parasite diversity and movement.

II. STRATEGY

1. Introduction

When it was launched in 2005, the goal of PMI was to reduce malaria-related mortality by 50% across 15 high-burden countries in sub-Saharan Africa through a rapid scale-up of four proven and highly effective malaria prevention and treatment measures: insecticide-treated mosquito nets (ITNs); indoor residual spraying (IRS); accurate diagnosis and prompt treatment with artemisinin-based combination therapies (ACTs); and intermittent preventive treatment for pregnant women (IPTp). With the passage of the Tom Lantos and Henry J. Hyde Global Leadership against HIV/AIDS, Tuberculosis, and Malaria Act in 2008, PMI developed a U.S. Government Malaria Strategy for 2009–2014. This strategy included a long-term vision for malaria control in which sustained high coverage with malaria prevention and treatment interventions would progressively lead to malaria-free zones in Africa, with the ultimate goal of worldwide malaria eradication by 2040-2050. Consistent with this strategy and the increase in annual appropriations supporting PMI, four new sub-Saharan African countries and one regional program in the Greater Mekong Subregion of Southeast Asia were added in 2011. The contributions of PMI, together with those of other partners, have led to dramatic improvements in the coverage of malaria control interventions in PMI-supported countries, and all 15 original countries have documented substantial declines in all-cause mortality rates among children less than five years of age.

In 2015, PMI launched the next six-year strategy, setting forth a bold and ambitious goal and objectives. The PMI Strategy 2015-2020 takes into account the progress over the past decade and the new challenges that have arisen. Malaria prevention and control remains a major U.S. foreign assistance objective and PMI's Strategy fully aligns with the U.S. Government's vision of ending preventable child and maternal deaths and ending extreme poverty. It is also in line with the goals articulated in the RBM Partnership's second generation global malaria action plan, *Action and Investment to defeat Malaria (AIM) 2016-2030: for a Malaria-Free World* and WHO's updated Global Technical Strategy: 2016-2030. Under the PMI Strategy 2015-2020, the U.S. Government's goal is to work with PMI-supported countries and partners to further reduce malaria deaths and substantially decrease malaria morbidity, towards the long-term goal of elimination.

Senegal was selected as a PMI country in fiscal year (FY) 2007. Large-scale implementation of ACTs and rapid diagnostic tests (RDTs) began in 2007 and progressed rapidly with support from PMI and other partners. ACTs and IPTp are now available in all public health facilities nationwide, RDTs are used to confirm malaria cases at all levels of the health system (including the community level) and 10.7 million long-lasting insecticide-treated bed nets (LLINs) have been distributed using a universal coverage approach since 2010.

This FY 2016 Malaria Operational Plan presents a detailed implementation plan for Senegal, based on the strategies of PMI and the National Malaria Control Program (NMCP). It was developed in consultation with the NMCP and with the participation of national and international partners involved in malaria prevention and control in the country. The activities that PMI is proposing to support fit in well with the National Malaria Control strategy and plan and build on investments made by PMI and other partners to improve and expand malaria-related services, including the Global Fund to Fight AIDS, Tuberculosis, and Malaria (Global Fund) malaria grants. This document briefly reviews the current status of malaria control policies and interventions in Senegal, describes progress to date, identifies challenges and unmet needs to achieving the targets of the NMCP and PMI, and provides a description of activities that are planned with FY 2016 funding.

2. Malaria situation in Senegal

Senegal's estimated population in 2016 will be approximately 14.3 million, based on the most recent census conducted in 2013. Although substantial improvements have been achieved since the 1960s, Senegal's indicators of human development remain low, with the country ranked 163 out of 187 countries worldwide on the Human Development Index[1]. The infant mortality rate is 33 deaths per 1,000 live births and the under-five mortality rate is 54 deaths per 1,000 live births[2]. Maternal mortality ratio is estimated to be 370 deaths per 100,000 live births and the life expectancy at birth is 63 years[1]. The adult HIV prevalence rate is estimated at 0.5% for adults 15-49 years of age, with 15,000 adults and 5,400 children (aged 0 to 14) estimated to be living with HIV/AIDS[1].

Malaria is endemic throughout Senegal and 100% of the population is at risk of the disease. The three ecological zones, based on annual rainfall, are the northern Sahelian zone with < 400 mm of rainfall occurring between July and September, the central Sahelian zone with 400 – 1,000 mm of rainfall occurring between July and October, and the southern tropical zone with 1,000 – 1,250 mm of rainfall occurring between June and October. The country can also be divided into two epidemiological zones: the tropical zone, with year-round transmission peaking during the rainy season and lower transmission during the rest of the year; and the Sahelian zone, with high transmission toward the end of and immediately after the rainy season and very low transmission during the rest of the year. Transmission in the Sahelian zone may occur throughout the year, often as small outbreaks, in areas close to rivers or other water sources that persist through the dry season. In peri-urban areas, persistent flooding during and after the rainy season has led to higher peaks in transmission during the rainy season and a longer transmission season. *Plasmodium falciparum* is the major malaria parasite species, accounting for more than 90% of all infections. The main vector species are *Anopheles gambiae sensu strictu, An. coluzzii, An. arabiensis, An. funestus,* and *An. melas.* The species distribution depends on rainfall and the presence of permanent sources of water.

The vulnerable groups in Senegal comprise an estimated 2.75 million children under five and 572,000 pregnant women. According to routine data collected by the NMCP between 2001 and 2006, malaria was responsible for just over one-third of all outpatient consultations. In October 2007, the case definition of malaria changed from a purely clinical definition to one that relies on parasitological confirmation. From that point on, health workers were directed to test all suspected cases of malaria and to treat and report only those cases with positive results. Suspected cases of malaria were defined as those with fever who do not have signs or symptoms

---

[1] 2014 Human Development Index, United Nations Development Programme: http://hdr.undp.org/en
[2] 2014 Continuous DHS Senegal: http://dhsprogram.com/what-we-do/survey/survey-display-457.cfm

indicative of other illnesses. In 2013, 87% of suspected cases were tested, and in 2014, 96% were tested.

As a result of these changes, the proportion of all outpatient visits due to malaria fell from 36% (clinically diagnosed) in 2001 to 6% (parasitologically confirmed) in 2008. The proportion of all deaths in children under five in health facilities that were attributed to malaria also fell from 30% to 7% over the same timeframe. Although the change in the case definition of malaria obscured assessment of the impact of program activities, this reduction continued between 2008 and 2009, with malaria representing only 3% of all outpatient visits and 4% of all deaths in 2009. Morbidity and mortality data were not available between 2010 and 2012 because health worker unions were staging a nationwide data retention strike. This data strike ended in March 2013, and data have been backfilled, though data quality for 2010-2012 is not optimal. In 2013, the routine data system was functional once again. Incidence of confirmed malaria per thousand increased from 14 in 2009 to 27 in 2013, but fell to 19 in 2014. Incidence ranged from 1 per 1,000 in five northern districts to over 200 per 1,000 in two southeastern districts.

In 2015, the NMCP adopted an updated policy of testing all patients under the age of five with fever, regardless of any other signs or symptoms. Given the uncertainty in the true number of patients with fever, this transition will be gradual to avoid wide scale stockouts of commodities. In those over five years of age, all febrile patients will be tested from July to January, with the previous algorithm (those with fever who do not have signs or symptoms indicative of other illnesses) in use from February to June. In 2016, all febrile patients, regardless of age, season, or other symptoms will be tested with an RDT.

3. Country health system delivery structure and Ministry of Health (MoH) organization

Administratively, the country is divided into 14 regions and 46 departments. The health system functions at the level of the regions (each with a Regional Chief Medical Officer) and is further decentralized into 76 health districts that may be all or part of an administrative department. Health districts are led by the District Chief Medical Officer who, together with the District Health Management Team, oversees care and treatment activities at the District Health Center and at peripheral facilities, as well as prevention activities. Health districts have at least one health center and a number of health posts that are staffed by chief nurses and sometimes midwives. There are approximately 1,247 health posts in Senegal.

Although not a formal part of the health system, Senegal's health care pyramid rests on a foundation of approximately 2,162 functional health huts that are established and managed by local communities and cover approximately 50% of the country's population. A functional health hut is defined as one that has a trained community health worker (literacy is preferred but not required), regular supervision by the chief nurse of the health post, and the basic structure and equipment needed to provide services. Malaria case management with free RDTs and ACTs was rolled out in health huts in 2008. The community health workers (CHWs) offer an integrated package of preventive and curative services or referral for more advanced medical care. Additional community health staff includes *matrones*, who are trained birth attendants, and *relais*, who are health educators and communicators.

Since 2008, a new type of health worker, the village malaria worker (*dispensateur de soins à domicile - DSDOM*), provides testing with RDTs and treatment with ACTs through the home-based management of malaria program (*prise en charge à domicile - PECADOM*), now active in 1,992 villages in 13 regions where health services are difficult to access. In 2012, 88 DSDOMs were trained in management of pneumonia and diarrhea in addition to malaria, an approach called integrated PECADOM that was scaled up to 492 DSDOMs in the Kédougou and Tambacounda regions in 2013 and to 1,267 villages in 7 regions in 2014. Both health huts and DSDOMs are linked to their supervising health post by the commodity supply chain and the health information system (i.e., they receive supplies from and submit data to the health post). In 2014, the Ministry of Health adopted a National Strategic Plan for Community Health to improve linkages between the community level and the formal health system, increase ownership by communities, and improve coordination of activities to make Senegal a model for community health.

4. National malaria control strategy: Achieve pre-elimination by 2018

In developing the 2011-2015 National Strategic Plan, the NMCP adopted a goal of reaching the threshold for pre-elimination (defined by the NMCP as annual incidence <5 cases per 1,000) by 2015, continuing the use of proven interventions already scaled up nationally, adopting new proven interventions in a targeted manner, and piloting new interventions. In 2013, the NMCP conducted a midterm program review. Key findings included the need for closer collaboration with private health care providers (case management and reporting) and private enterprises (coordination and resource mobilization); weaknesses in stock management at all levels, including providing malaria commodities free of charge; and the need to extend weekly surveillance to all low-transmission districts. The National Strategic Plan was subsequently updated. In early 2014, the decision was made to develop a new Strategic Framework that would guide the development of a concept note for the Global Fund, covering activities expected to be implemented from 2015 through 2017 (the Framework goes through 2018 in alignment with the National Health Development Plan). The goal of reaching pre-elimination has been extended to 2018, with interventions targeted to the different transmission zones. In addition to the standard interventions, pre-elimination zones are eligible for case investigation and reactive case detection, while the highest transmission regions (control zones) receive seasonal malaria chemoprevention (SMC) and are prioritized for active home-based management (PECADOM Plus) (see map, below).

Interventions targeted to incidence, by district (Strategic Framework 2014-2018)

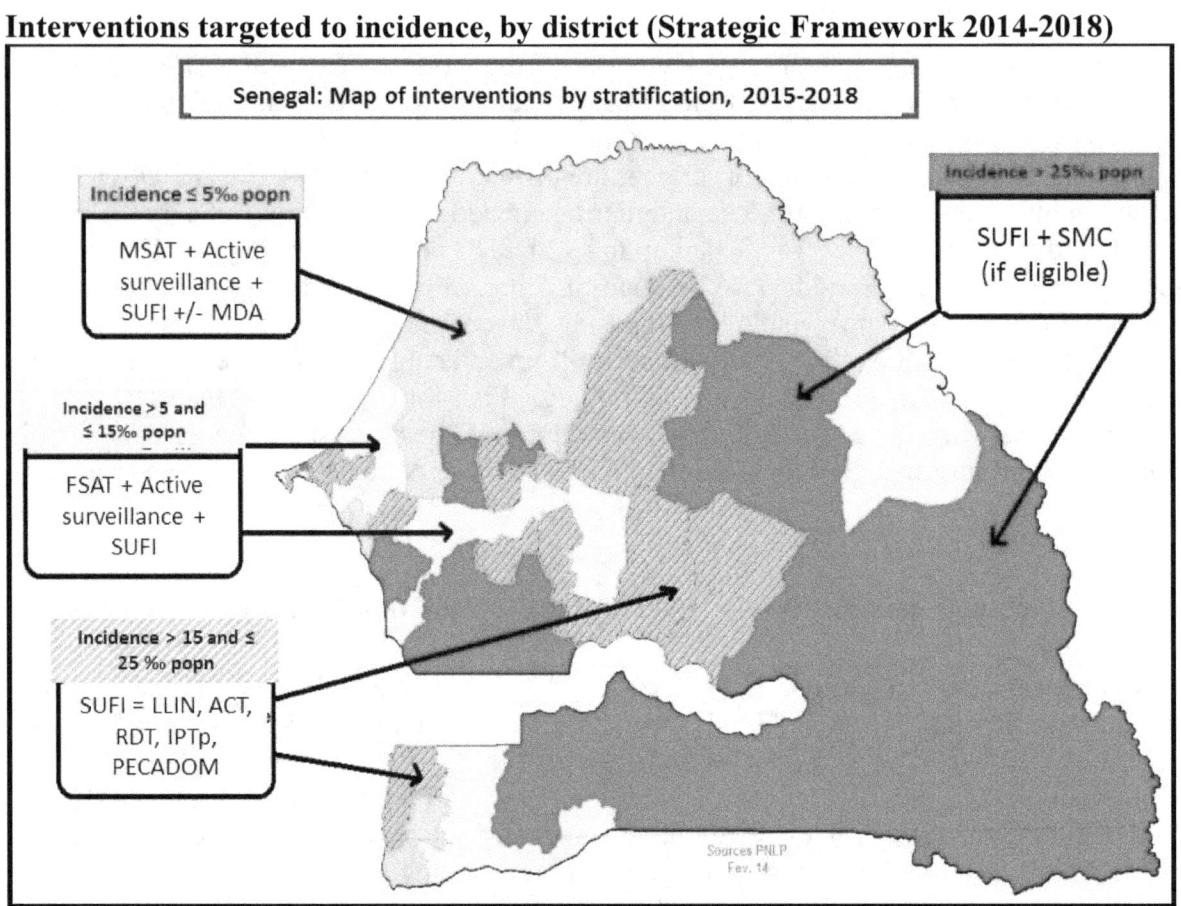

MSAT – mass screen and treat; FSAT - focal screen and treat; SUFI – scale up for impact (LLINs, IPTp, RDTs, ACTs, PECADOM Plus); MDA – mass drug administration; SMC – seasonal malaria chemoprevention.
Source: National Malaria Control Strategic Framework (2014-2018)
Note: MSAT and MDA are MACEPA and UCAD research projects.

NMCP strategy by intervention

Senegal has now adopted all the WHO-recommended interventions and remains a leader in piloting and scaling up new recommendations and innovative strategies to increase the reach and effectiveness of interventions. The 2014-2018 Strategic Framework outlines the following package of activities:

- **LLINs**: Mass distribution for universal coverage transitioning to a nationwide campaign in 2016, with scale-up of multi-channel routine distribution.
- **IRS**: Focal spraying to target hotspots at the level of the health post in districts with annual incidence greater than 30 per 1,000.
- **Larval source management**: Bio-larvicides applied in areas where larval sources are few, fixed, and findable, such as the suburbs of Dakar or dry areas where water holes are known.
- **Seasonal malaria chemoprevention**: One treatment of sulfadoxine-pyrimethamine (SP) and amodiaquine (AQ) monthly during the transmission season, up to four months, for children 3-120 months in regions that meet WHO criteria.

- **Malaria in pregnancy**: IPTp with SP under directly observed therapy, beginning during the second trimester, at every contact with the health facility, at intervals of at least one month. Every pregnant woman is to receive a free LLIN during her first antenatal care (ANC) visit. Pregnant women with confirmed malaria are treated with quinine in the first trimester and with ACTs thereafter, unless signs of severe disease, when IV quinine or artesunate is used.
- **Case management**
  - Uncomplicated malaria: All suspected cases are to be confirmed with RDT, and patients with positive tests treated with an ACT. Artemether-lumefantrine, artesunate-amodiaquine, and dihydroartemisinin-piperaquine are co-first line therapies.
  - Severe disease: Pre-referral treatment with rectal artesunate if identified at community or health post level. Definitive treatment at the health center or hospital level with IV quinine or artesunate, to be followed with a course of oral ACT. Hospitalized patients should have malaria confirmed by blood smear.
  - Community level: All patients with fever are tested with an RDT and patients with positive tests receive an ACT. Both health hut and home-based care programs are integrated with diarrhea and pneumonia.
- **Health promotion**: Evidence-based behavior change campaigns and activities accompanied by M&E to measure impact, increasing role of communities and private sector.
- **Epidemic surveillance and response**: Epidemic surveillance sites report all data weekly and data are analyzed to identify hotspots. Case notification and reactive case investigation in pre-elimination zones.
- **Monitoring and evaluation/research**
  - Integration of NMCP data into DHIS2 adopted by the MoH, with quarterly data reviews.
  - Introduction of mobile health (mHealth) system to facilitate reporting of data at community level and reporting of weekly case counts.
  - Health facility supervision using tablet computers to streamline analysis and feedback.
  - Reinforce pharmacovigilance.
  - Operational research on the introduction of low-dose primaquine for transmission reduction in elimination settings.
- **Supply chain management**: Improve storage and transport capacity, strengthen coordination between the NMCP and the Central Medical Stores (CMS), strengthen capacity for supply chain management at all levels, monitor drug quality and efficacy
- **Program management and coordination**: Improve managerial and operational capacity, increase resource mobilization and coordination efforts, and strengthen partnerships.

5. Updates in the strategy section

- Adoption of new diagnostic strategy with transition to testing of all patients with fever or history of fever in 2017. During 2016, all children under five years of age will be tested all year, and all patients above five years of age with fever during July – January will be tested, with the previous diagnostic algorithm (those with fever who do not have signs or symptoms indicative of other illnesses) applied to patients five years and older during February to June.

6. Integration, collaboration, and coordination

A coordination body was created in 2011, called the *Cadre de Concertation des Partenaires de Lutte contre le Paludisme,* which brings together funding, technical, and non-governmental partners. The president is selected on a rotating basis from among the partners, with the NMCP functioning as the secretariat. This group meets several times each year to exchange information and has been instrumental in helping resolve challenges and coordinate efforts.

Funding and technical partnerships

Senegal currently has one active **Global Fund** malaria grant for approximately $88 million, awarded to two principal recipients, the NMCP and IntraHealth International. Phase 1 of the grant was extended to the end of 2014 and the NMCP submitted a concept note in June 2014 under the new funding model for additional resources to cover the period 2015 to 2017, which is now being implemented. The NMCP, PMI, and Global Fund Senegal teams enjoy frequent communication and close collaboration.

The **World Bank** provides support for malaria through the Senegal River Basin Development Organization and the Nutrition Enhancement Project. Activities include LLIN distribution and communication/education.

The **World Health Organization** (WHO) provides limited technical and financial support for the implementation of treatment and prevention policies, planning, M&E, research, surveillance, and management of the NMCP.

The **United Nations Children's Fund** (UNICEF) provides support for district-level health plans in the regions of Kolda, Sédhiou, Kédougou, Tambacounda, and Matam. UNICEF collaborates with the United States Agency for International Development (USAID)-funded Community Health Program Component to support various community health interventions in more than 500 health huts. They also contributed to the scale-up of integrated PECADOM in four regions, and supported some operational costs for the 2013 SMC campaign (funding given by the Japan International Cooperation Agency (JICA)).

The **Islamic Development Bank** (IDB) provided $8 million in loans in 2009-2010 for the procurement of LLINs and RDTs, health personnel training, and supervision. They are finalizing a new $10 million loan to be disbursed beginning in 2015.

In addition to multilateral institutions, Senegal benefits from the support of various bilateral donors. The **French Cooperation** contributes to research activities through the *Institut Pasteur Dakar* and the *Institut de Recherche pour le Développement* (IRD) and places a technical advisor at the MoH. **JICA** and USAID have developed a joint partnership in Tambacounda and Kédougou regions; JICA donated $1 million for malaria activities in these regions through UNICEF in 2013. The **Chinese Cooperation** makes periodic donations of drugs for the treatment of uncomplicated and severe malaria, and the **Embassy of Thailand** has supported the participation of health personnel at malaria training courses in Thailand. The **Belgian Technical**

Cooperation is supporting the overall development of the health sector primarily in Fatick and Kaolack regions.

Senegal's non-governmental and faith-based partners are also numerous. *Medicos del Mundo* and several Spanish non-governmental organizations are active in Sédhiou and Kolda regions. They have supported outreach activities by health post staff, rehabilitation of health huts, and LLIN distribution campaign operations.

Speak Up Africa is a local non-governmental organization dedicated to mobilizing African leadership, resources, and individual action against malaria, diarrhea, and pneumonia in several countries. In Senegal, the group has supported various communications/advocacy activities and helps to draw in national celebrities to support the malaria control cause.

The **International Committee of the Red Cross** supports outreach activities and LLIN distribution campaign operations in conflict zones in Ziguinchor and Sédhiou regions, as well as in the mining areas of Kédougou Region.

The **Malaria Control and Evaluation Partnership for Africa** (MACEPA), which began work in Senegal in 2009, has implemented a pre-elimination project in one northern district, including enhanced and integrated surveillance and case investigation, and a mass screen and treat program in hotspots in three additional districts.

Senegal is fortunate to have strong academic and research capacities in epidemiology, parasitology and entomology at the NMCP, *Université Cheikh Anta Diop* (UCAD), the **Parasite Control Service (*Service de Lutte Anti-Parasitaire*), *Institut de Recherche et Développement* (IRD)**, and the *Institut Pasteur Dakar*. These groups have strong collaborative relationships and together have published much of the recent literature on malaria in Senegal.

Private sector

In recent years the NMCP has been working with an increasing number of private enterprises on outreach and sensitization programs, LLIN distributions, and malaria case management. For example, collaboration with the **Senegalese Sugar Company** in the northern city of Richard Toll led the company to introduce RDTs in their clinic, to screen all seasonal workers for malaria, and to provide them with LLINs. The company continues to be active in pre-elimination activities in the district, which was highlighted during 2014 World Malaria Day events. **BICIS Bank** (BNP/Paribas) has become more active in the past year, supporting the printing of a popular children's comic book on malaria and airing spots/messages on the video screens in their branches. The fuel company **Total** has supported communications activities and will sell socially marketed LLINs in their stations' shops. Nevertheless, meaningful, longer-term partnerships have proven to be challenging due to the time commitment and skills required to develop them.

Within United States Government (USG)

The **United States Peace Corps** and PMI embarked on a new partnership in 2011. In Senegal, PMI staff and implementing partners continue to regularly participate in pre-service and in-service training sessions and over the past year supported one third-year malaria volunteer to oversee malaria PCV malaria activities and liaise with PMI. Peace Corps volunteers also support PMI and the NMCP through information, education and communication (IEC) activities and by participating in M&E and operational research (OR) activities. Two innovative strategies piloted by Peace Corps, universal coverage distribution of LLINs targeting every sleeping space, and PECADOM Plus, a community-based active fever detection program, have been adopted by the NMCP.

7. PMI goal, objectives, strategic areas, and key indicators

Under the PMI Strategy for 2015-2020, the U.S. Government's goal is to work with PMI-supported countries and partners to further reduce malaria deaths and substantially decrease malaria morbidity, towards the long-term goal of elimination. Building upon the progress to date in PMI-supported countries, PMI will work with NMCPs and partners to accomplish the following objectives by 2020:

1. Reduce malaria mortality by one-third from 2015 levels in PMI-supported countries, achieving a greater than 80% reduction from PMI's original 2000 baseline levels.

2. Reduce malaria morbidity in PMI-supported countries by 40% from 2015 levels.

3. Assist at least five PMI-supported countries to meet the World Health Organization's (WHO) criteria for national or sub-national pre-elimination.[3]

These objectives will be accomplished by emphasizing five core areas of strategic focus:
1. Achieving and sustaining scale of proven interventions
2. Adapting to changing epidemiology and incorporating new tools
3. Improving countries' capacity to collect and use information
4. Mitigating risk against the current malaria control gains
5. Building capacity and health systems towards full country ownership

To track progress toward achieving and sustaining scale of proven interventions (area of strategic focus #1), PMI will continue to track the key indicators recommended by the Roll Back Malaria Monitoring and Evaluation Reference Group (RBM MERG) as listed below:

- Proportion of households with at least one ITN
- Proportion of households with at least one ITN for every two people
- Proportion of children under five years old who slept under an ITN the previous night
- Proportion of pregnant women who slept under an ITN the previous night
- Proportion of households in targeted districts protected by IRS
- Proportion of children under five years old with fever in the last two weeks for whom advice or treatment was sought
- Proportion of children under five with fever in the last two weeks who had a finger or heel stick

---

[3] http://whqlibdoc.who.int/publications/2007/9789241596084_eng.pdf

- Proportion receiving an ACT among children under five years old with fever in the last two weeks who received any antimalarial drugs
- Proportion of women who received two or more doses of IPTp for malaria during ANC visits during their last pregnancy

8. Progress on coverage/impact indicators to date

The table below shows that steady progress has been made for most malaria indicators in Senegal from 2005 until 2010, as measured by two Demographic and Health Surveys (DHS) (2005 and 2010), the first two rounds of the continuous DHS (2012-2013 and 2014), and two malaria indicator surveys (MISs) (2006 and 2008). While increase in coverage indicators has stalled, parasite prevalence, anemia, and all-cause mortality continue to fall. Of note, most of the surveys have taken place primarily during the dry season, when ITN use and parasitemia are generally lower, though this should not affect ITN ownership, IRS, and IPTp coverage, or child mortality.

Household ownership of at least one ITN rose from 20% in 2005 to 74% in 2014. Intra-household access to an ITN increased from 11% in 2005 to 63% in 2012. Utilization of ITNs by children under five rose from 7% in 2006 to 43% in 2014. Similar trends in utilization were observed with pregnant women and in the general population.

The proportion of pregnant women receiving two doses of IPTp with sulfadoxine-pyrimethamine (SP) increased from 12% in 2005 to 52% in 2008, but fell to 39% in 2010 due primarily to stockouts of SP, rising slightly to 41% in 2012 and remaining stable in 2014. Comparing the proportion of children with fever who received prompt treatment with an ACT across the surveys is difficult given the introduction of RDTs in late 2007 and the falling incidence, with treatment being given only to patients with a positive test. In addition, the diagnostic algorithm mandated that only those without an obvious alternate cause for fever be tested with an RDT. In 2014, 11% of children had a fever in the last two weeks, 0.3% of which received an ACT within 24 hours.

As a result of the scale-up of malaria control interventions, parasitemia in children under five has fallen from 6% nationwide in 2008 to 1.2% nationwide in 2014. The mortality rate for children under five has fallen from 121 deaths per 1,000 live births in the 2005 DHS to 54 in the 2014 cDHS. These indicators are available at the national level annually through the continuous Demographic and Health Survey (cDHS).

Table 1: Evolution of Key Malaria Indicators in Senegal from 2005 to 2014

Indicator	2005 DHS	2006 MIS	2008 MIS	2010 DHS	2012-3 cDHS	2014 cDHS
% Households with an ITN	20	36	60	63	73	74
% Households with at least one ITN for every two people	11	19	36	41	30	36
% General population who slept under an ITN the previous night	6	12	23	29	41	40
% Children under five who slept under an ITN the previous night	7	16	29	35	46	43
% Pregnant women who slept under an ITN the previous night	9	17	29	37	43	38
% Households with an ITN or sprayed within previous 12 months	--	--	--	66	76	76
% Women who received two or more doses of IPTp during their last pregnancy in the last two years	12	49	52	39	41	40
% Children under five years old with fever in the last two weeks for whom advice or treatment was sought	40	--	--	44		54
% Children under five with fever in the last two weeks who received a diagnostic test	--	--	9	10	15	12
% Children under five with fever in the last two weeks who received treatment with an ACT within 24 hours of onset of fever	--	3	2	3	0.5	0.3
% Women of childbearing age with anemia (<11 g/dL)	59	--	64	54	--	--
% Children 6-59 months with severe anemia (<8 g/dL)	20	--	17	14	10	5.3
% Children under five with parasitemia (*P. falciparum*)	--	--	6	3	3	1.2
Under-five mortality rate per 1,000 live births	121	--	85	72	65	54

9. Other relevant evidence on progress

The Impact Evaluation, which covered the period from 2006-2010, was completed in late 2013. All-cause under-five child mortality fell 40% during that period, coinciding with dramatic increases in coverage of ITNs and IPTp and a 50% decrease in malaria parasite prevalence. Strikingly, the most dramatic decreases in mortality were seen in the populations in which the increases in intervention coverage and decreases in parasite prevalence were the most pronounced: in the southeastern regions, in the poorest three quintiles, and in rural populations, suggesting that the decrease in mortality correlated with increase in intervention coverage and decrease in parasite prevalence. Routine data corroborated the picture from nationwide surveys, demonstrating a dramatic decrease in confirmed malaria cases and deaths due to malaria, even as the numbers of total consultations and total hospitalizations increased, suggesting a simultaneous increase in access to health services.

While parasite prevalence among children under the age of five remained stable at 3% from 2010 to 2012, routine data available in 2013 show an increase in incidence from 14 per 1,000 in 2009 to 27 per 1,000 in 2013, with the most pronounced increase in the southeast. The many contributing factors include: increased access to care and/or increased data completeness, particularly at the community level (342% increase in consultations reported by the community level from 2010 to 2013), with a 23% increase in total consultations among children under five from 2010 to 2013; increased rainfall; and degradation and attrition of LLINs distributed in 2010 in the four southeastern regions that were scheduled to have been replaced prior to the rainy season in 2013. In comparison, in the regions in which universal coverage was conducted in early 2013 (Dakar and Thiès), incidence dramatically decreased. In 2014, a dry year, incidence fell to 18 per 1,000, with the greatest decreases in the regions in which seasonal malaria chemoprevention was implemented for the first time in 2014, and parasite prevalence among children under five years in the cDHS fell to 1.2%

The NMCP identified the need to repeat a similar exercise to study and document the achievements in malaria control for the period 2011-2015. This second Impact Evaluation will be conducted during 2016 and funding for this activity in included in the FY 2015 Malaria Operational Plan.

10. Challenges and opportunities

Senegal has made great strides against malaria in the last decade, though challenges remain in virtually every domain of malaria prevention and treatment. Recent policy changes and innovative solutions being piloted provide opportunities to advance malaria control.

Challenges

Pharmaceutical management: Management challenges at the c, including delays in procuring and distributing essential medications, inadequate quantification, and poor responsiveness to program needs, represent a significant threat to successful program implementation. There are positive signs from the leadership of the CMS, but periodic stockouts continue at community and local levels, and occasionally at regional and district levels. There are concerns that pharmacy managers, from the CMS to the health post level, neglect free commodities (such as ACTs, RDTs, and SP) in favor of those that bring in revenue. In addition, there are very few professional pharmacists or logisticians below the Regional Pharmacy level, meaning that this critical function simply does not get the attention that it requires.

Data quality and timeliness: Historically, Senegal has had a very robust routine malaria information system. However, the data retention strike meant that for three years the NMCP had no information on the number of suspected malaria cases, diagnostic tests performed, or confirmed cases. The data strike was formally lifted in March 2013, although it continues in a handful of districts, and the process of rebuilding the routine health information system is underway. The Ministry of Health is mobilizing to implement the DHIS2 and develop an integrated mHealth strategy, which the NMCP will also adopt. Until then, the NMCP receives data from the districts during the quarterly data reviews. Completeness of reporting, particularly inclusion of community level data, is variable. The NMCP is piloting mobile tools to assist with weekly case reporting, stock management, and community level reporting. The use and interpretation of the data with community level reporting will have to be looked at carefully since the inclusion of the number of cases detected at the community level is expected to increase the number of cases reported and therefore impact the calculations of reported incidence.

Insecticide resistance: Insecticide resistance threatens both LLIN and IRS programs in Senegal, as it does in many PMI countries. Only 3 of the 15 surveillance sites showed sensitivity to pyrethroids in 2010 and none were in districts targeted for IRS. While pyrethroid sensitivity has increased in many of the monitored districts, both in those sprayed with carbamates and those not, a return to pyrethroids for IRS is not foreseen given the strategy of universal coverage with LLINs. Carbamates were used in all IRS districts from 2011-2013, though their short life (two months) has necessitated a switch to organophosphates in the higher transmission districts with longer rainy seasons. Susceptibility to carbamates and organophosphates remained high in 2014 in most districts where testing was done.

Opportunities

WHO policy adoption: Senegal has adopted all WHO-recommended interventions pertinent to the Senegalese context. The implementation of the new recommendations for SMC and for severe disease management may have a dramatic impact on morbidity and mortality due to malaria in the upcoming years. The NMCP is committed to leadership in the region, piloting and evaluating new strategies including active case detection, introduction of single low-dose primaquine for transmission reduction in elimination areas, and weekly case reporting.

Continuous Survey: Senegal is the first sub-Saharan African country to pilot a continuous survey, implementation of which began in October 2012, during the high transmission season. The continuous survey includes both population-based (DHS) and health facility (service provision assessment (SPA) components. While balancing the needs of malaria and other programs is challenging, the continuous survey presents an opportunity to measure trends that will guide decision-making on a more frequent basis. PMI has worked with the implementing partner to ensure that the sampling strategy takes into account the strongly seasonal transmission and assures the comparability of regions (For cDHS results, please refer to Table 1 in the Progress to date section and Table 2 in the ITN section).

Collaboration with Peace Corps: The local partnership with Peace Corps continues to be solidified through development of a package of malaria activities from which volunteers may choose. In 2013, a third year volunteer was recruited to provide assistance with data management for entomological monitoring at UCAD. In addition, Peace Corps volunteers in Saraya District collaborated with the NMCP and the district health office to implement an active version of the PECADOM program, called PECADOM Plus. The DSDOMs conducted weekly door-to-door sweeps to identify people with fever, test them with RDTs, and treat positive cases. This strategy is being adopted by the NMCP for further scale-up. The more than 200 volunteers in-country represent a valuable resource for everything from testing communications materials to conducting household visits to gathering information on specific questions. In return, the PMI Resident Advisors provide technical assistance on specific volunteer projects, facilitate training sessions, and ensure that Peace Corps leadership has a place at the table when key malaria interventions are being planned and implemented.

Direct funding: USAID's procurement reforms have given PMI/Senegal the opportunity to directly support its two strongest local partners – the NMCP and UCAD. Previously, PMI channeled funds for these partners through WHO. Starting in FY 2012, PMI negotiated fixed amount reimbursement agreements with both entities to fund specific activities. The principal of payment based on the achievement of milestones has given PMI the opportunity to focus on defining high-level results and to encourage our partners to think strategically about how to accomplish them. These two agreements have been very successful to date, and a new agreement with the National Drug Control Laboratory is in the process of being established. While a very successful program, it is also enormously time consuming to oversee. Process delays have impacted the timely implementation of activities that support the country's malaria control strategy.

III. OPERATIONAL PLAN

PMI supports all of the major elements of the NMCP's 2014-2018 Strategic Framework, with the exception of larval source management.

1. Insecticide-treated nets

NMCP/PMI objectives

The NMCP 2014-2018 Strategic Framework includes one overarching strategy for malaria prevention related to LLINs, which is to strengthen distribution mechanisms. It describes two distinct approaches: 1) mass distribution of LLINs to achieve/maintain universal coverage, defined as one insecticide-treated net per sleeping space; and 2) routine distribution to allow ongoing access to LLINs. The objective is for 80% of the population to sleep under an LLIN.

Progress since PMI was launched

The NMCP and partners have supported various approaches for LLIN distribution:

1) **Periodic mass free distribution of LLINs:** In 2007, the NMCP began implementing large-scale mass "catch-up" distributions of LLINs to children under five, culminating in a national campaign in 2009. Universal coverage distributions targeting every sleeping space began in 2010 and were completed in April 2013, with 6.9 million LLINs distributed. This rolling universal coverage campaign restarted in 2013 in Kédougou, and to date has re-covered the 8 regions covered in 2010 and 2011 during the first universal coverage campaign, distributing 3.8 million LLINs from July 2013 to November 2014.

2) **Routine distributions:**
   a. **LLINs for pregnant women:** During 2008 and 2009, PMI supported the subsidized sale of LLINs and later LLINs to pregnant women and children under five. This system involved agreements between facility health committees and private sector net distributors, with beneficiaries contributing a small copayment. Beginning in July 2012, free nets were made available to pregnant women during their first antenatal consultation. During 2014, 105,686 LLINs were distributed to pregnant women.

   b. **Free distribution in schools**: In 2013, PMI piloted free distribution to primary school students in two regions, with 75,710 LLINs distributed in classes CI and CE2 (six- and nine-year olds) once during the school year. The distributions were accompanied by educational activities. Two additional regions were added in 2014 and 135,117 nets were distributed in 2014.

   c. **Untargeted sales of subsidized bed nets:** From 2006 to 2007, the NMCP supported bed net sales to the general population at health facility pharmacies and through community-based organizations (CBOs) at a subsidized price of 1,000 West African Financial Community Francs (CFA) (about $2 per net), a portion of which was retained by the health districts and CBOs, a policy continued by PMI until 2010. Beginning in July 2012, PMI began supporting a system to make subsidized nets available to all clients frequenting health facilities at a price of 500 F CFA (about $1).

d. PMI expanded the availability of subsidized nets in 2013 by supporting a pilot in two regions using CBOs. Community "relays" distribute coupons during home visits or from a fixed point and individuals then redeem the coupons at distribution sites. As with the health facility channel, the LLINs are sold for 500 F CFA (approximately $1) and the copay is shared at different levels to cover transport costs and communications activities.

e. Finally, PMI supports a social marketing program in pharmacies and other retail outlets. These nets are sold at a price of 1,000 F CFA and are branded with a unique logo and promoted through a communications campaign that focuses on being a protective head of household. PMI provides the LLINs to pharmaceutical wholesalers, who then assure distribution through their normal supply chain. Actors at each level of the supply chain retain the profit from the sale of LLINs to cover their operational costs and communications activities.

3) **Commercial sales to the general public:** PMI supported social marketing of full-price LLINs in the private sector from 2007 to 2009. When mass free distributions began, however, the market was significantly weakened. Full-price LLINs can still be found in pharmacies and some shops, primarily in major urban areas, but they are generally not long-lasting varieties. These bed nets are sold at 3,000 – 7,500 F CFA ($6 – $15) each.

As a result of implementing these different strategies, household ownership of at least one ITN has increased substantially (from 20% in 2005 to 73% in 2012 and 74% in 2014). Utilization of ITNs by children under five rose from 7% in 2005 to 46% in 2012 with a slight decrease in 2014 (43%), with similar trends observed among pregnant women and in the general population. However, these data mask significant disparities among regions, reflecting socio-cultural differences as well as the progression of the universal coverage campaign (see Table 2). For example, the West zone, which includes the populous and urbanized regions of Dakar and Thiès, had not yet been covered by the campaign at the time of data collection for the 2012 continuous survey but received nets in 2013. Net ownership in this region increased by 12% in the 2014 cDHS. Possession of ITNs is highest among the poorest quintiles (greater than 83%), while use is highest for the middle income quintiles (43-49% for all households, 56-59% in households with at least one ITN).

Table 2: ITN possession and use by zone and population in 2013 and 2014

Zone - year	Proportion of households possessing at least 1 ITN	Average number of ITNs per household	Proportion of population that slept under an ITN the previous night			In households with at least 1 ITN, proportion of population that slept under an ITN the previous night		
			General popn	Children under 5	Pregnant women	General popn	Children under 5	Pregnant women
North 2013	93	3.7	61	64	64	65	67	68
2014	81	3.2	48	53	35	59	63	44
West 2013	50	1.7	24	19	24	41	45	34
2014	62	2.3	33	36	28	49	52	51
Center2013	88	3.9	48	50	47	54	57	51
2014	82	3.3	37	38	40	45	46	50
South 2013	86	3.2	40	43	45	47	50	52
2014	89	3.5	53	54	56	60	62	65

Source: 2012-13 cDHS and 2014 cDHS
Note: Due to the timing of the surveys, ITN use is measured during the dry season. Coverage estimates are therefore probably an underestimation of actual usage.

Progress during the last 12-18 months

Following completion of its national universal coverage campaign in April 2013, the NMCP restarted mass distributions in the regions that were initially covered in 2010. Kédougou and Kolda regions were completed in 2013 (July and November, respectively) and six more regions (Sédhiou and Tambacounda in June, and Diourbel, Fatick, Kaolack and Kaffrine in November) were covered in 2014 using Global Fund and JICA/UNICEF resources. A total of 3,319,204 LLINs were distributed in 2014 in these six regions. Due to delays in procuring Global Fund nets, PMI contributed 360,000 nets from its existing stock that were reimbursed when Global Fund nets arrived.

PMI continues to focus on the routine distribution system, although this has suffered in FY 2014 due to delays in the transfer of management responsibilities from an implementing partner to the NMCP and to availability of funding. The NMCP undertook a situational analysis in February 2014 to consolidate information on the number of LLINs distributed and existing stocks, lessons learned during implementation, and recommendations for expansion of the pilot programs. A "relaunch" plan was validated by the national coordinating committee in April 2014, which served as a roadmap for the following year. Key elements included: 1) eliminating coupons for the health facility and community channels to simplify the acquisition process and reduce bottlenecks related to supplying the coupons; 2) increasing the involvement of local authorities in identifying appropriate storage facilities; and 3) a plan for introducing the different channels in each region. School-based distributions continued in the two pilot regions (Louga and Ziguinchor) and two additional regions (Saint-Louis and Matam) that are not scheduled for another mass campaign until 2016.

The social marketing program received a boost last year from a partnership developed with *City Dia*, which operates grocery stores as well as the shops co-located with Total gas stations.

During FY 2014, more than 500,000 LLINs were distributed through the following channels:

Table 3. ITNs Distributed

Channel	FY 2014	FY 2015*
Health facility – ANC	93,495	57,614
Health facility – general consultations	222,053	134,882
Schools	134,805	891
CBOs	52,921	55,698
Social marketing (sold to distributors)	134,938	69,580
TOTAL	638,212	318,665

*Quantities for a partial year (October 2014 through May 2015)

PMI developed a protocol and began implementing durability monitoring in May 2015 for LLINs distributed during the 2014 mass campaigns in six regions.

Commodity gap analysis
Maintaining high LLIN coverage levels after the mass campaigns will require keeping up LLIN distribution via the different routine channels across the country. Approximately 1.8 million nets need to be distributed through the routine channels every year in order to maintain coverage. Under its new Strategic Framework, the NMCP has decided to stop the phased approach to mass campaigns and to implement a nationwide replacement campaign in 2016. The different routine channels will continue to operate, providing the population with several options for replacing worn out nets in the interim.

Table 4: LLIN Gap Analysis

Calendar Year	2015	2016[1]	2017
Total Population	**14,318,196**	**14,704,787**	**15,101,817**
Routine Distribution Needs			
Pregnant women during first prenatal care visit (3.9% of the population); assumes 100% attendance for one visit	558,410	286,743	588,971
Other health facility clients; assumes 4% of all clients will request an ITN	321,300	164,988	338,885
Community-based organizations	357,955	183,810	377,545
Primary school students	310,347	0	729,798
Social marketing	139,150	76,533	146,278
Estimated total need for routine channels	*1,687,162*	*712,064*	*2,181,477*
Mass Distribution Needs			
2016 national campaign		8,000,000	0
Estimated total need for mass campaigns		*8,000,000*	*0*
Total Routine and Mass ITN Needs	**1,687,162**	**8,712,064**	**2,181,477**
Partner Contributions			
PMI (primarily routine channels)	2,714,000[2]	1,047,120	1,200,000
Global Fund (mass distribution campaign only)		4,178,854	
Islamic Development Bank		1,300,000	
Senegal River Basin Development Organization		600,000	
Total Partner Contributions	**2,714,000**	**7,125,974**	**1,200,000**
Total ITN Surplus (Gap)	**1,026,838**	**(1,586,090)**	**(981,477)**

[1]Routine needs for 2016 estimated to be half of earlier years due to the national mass campaign occurring during 2016. [2] These LLINs are already in country.

PMI plans to provide approximately 1.2 million of the needed LLINs each year, which will be distributed primarily through the routine channels except in 2016. The surplus of PMI nets in 2016 will be used for the campaign. Global Fund is expected to procure approximately 4 million LLINs for the 2016 campaign and the nets provided by PMI will close the net gap. In the 2016 campaign the country plans to cover the whole country and thereafter, plans to rely on routine distribution channels to maintain coverage.

Plans and justification

With FY 2016 funds, PMI and the NMCP plan to focus efforts on maintaining a constant supply of nets and a strong, nationwide routine distribution system for LLINs as described above. PMI also plans to support communications activities to inform the population about mechanisms to acquire nets and their proper use and maintenance. These activities are described in the behavior change communication (BCC) section.

PMI will continue LLIN durability monitoring of nets distributed during the November 2014 mass campaigns, as well as conduct baseline and possibly follow-up monitoring for the nets distributed during the 2016 campaign, depending on when the campaign is implemented. Collections are scheduled for May 2015, November 2015, November 2016, and November 2017. Under this protocol, the same cohort of nets distributed in 2014 will be followed out to 2017.

Proposed activities with FY 2016 funding ($4,811,000)

1. *Procurement ($4,000,000) and operational support ($700,000) for distribution of LLINs*
PMI plans to support the routine LLIN distribution channels by procuring approximately 1.2 million LLINs and supporting operational costs. Operational costs for the routine system are expected to decrease significantly as the different channels will be fully functional nationwide, but will continue to include transportation to regions/districts and supervision.

2. *LLIN durability monitoring ($111,000)*
PMI will continue to support the routine monitoring of nets that were distributed in the 2014 campaigns in 6 regions (36 months after distribution). However, if the nationwide mass distribution of nets during the 2016 campaign makes it difficult to find and evaluate these nets, the funds will be used for the monitoring of the 2016 nets.

2. Indoor residual spraying

NMCP/PMI objectives

Senegal's 2014-2018 Strategic Framework includes IRS as a key component of malaria prevention along with other vector control interventions, such as LLINs and larval source management. The NMCP has adopted a targeted approach for IRS: a) districts with a yearly incidence of less than 30 per 1,000 will not receive IRS; b) districts with an incidence between 30 and 50 per 1,000 may have targeted IRS in the health post zones where malaria incidence is greater than 50 per 1,000 (hot spots); and c) districts with an incidence greater than 50 per 1,000 will receive IRS over the whole district. Routine health system data and entomological parameters such as indoor biting and resting rates will be used to assist in determination of where IRS may be appropriate. The goal for IRS is to protect at least 90% of the population in targeted areas.

Progress since PMI was launched

Senegal has benefitted from IRS since PMI began work in the country in 2007. The first three districts sprayed with PMI support—Richard Toll, Nioro, and Vélingara—each represented different ecological zones. One spray round was carried out just before the high transmission season in each district, while in Richard Toll, a district along the Senegal River, another round was done immediately prior to the second seasonal peak in April. After entomological monitoring demonstrated that the insecticidal activity persisted long enough to cover the second peak, this second round was eliminated in 2010. Also in 2010, IRS operations were expanded to Guinguinéo, Malem Hodar, and Koumpentoum, districts that were among the 16 health districts prioritized for IRS by the NMCP. In 2011, because malaria rates were low and insecticide resistance was high in Richard Toll, spray operations ceased in this district and Koungheul was selected as a replacement. In early 2013, the IRS Steering Committee made the decision to cease IRS operations in the districts of Guinguinéo and Nioro because data indicated that malaria rates had become very low. A plan for post-withdrawal action was prepared, including communications at both administrative and community levels and enhanced surveillance.

The population protected during the 7 years of IRS ranged from around 650,000 in 2007 to more than 1 million in 2012, with high coverage rates being achieved in most years (see Table 5 for last 4 years). As malaria incidence decreases, fewer health post zones in the districts targeted for IRS will meet the NMCP criteria for IRS, therefore the population covered will decrease.

Table 5: IRS Coverage

Year	Number of Districts Sprayed	Insecticide Used (# districts)	Number of Structures Sprayed	Coverage Rate	Population Protected
2012	6	Bendiocarb	306,916	98%	1,095,093
2013	4	Bendiocarb	206,704	98%	690,090
2014	4	Bendiocarb (2) Organophosphate (2)	204,159	97%	708,999
2015	4 (hot spots)	Bendiocarb (1) Organophosphate (3)	111,201*	97%	434,201*
2016	4 (hot spots)	Organophosphate	90,000**	TBD	300,000**
2017	TBD (hotspots)	Organophosphate	75,000**	TBD	250,000**

*Preliminary data as of August 2015
**Represents projected targets

Pyrethroids were used during the first four years of spray operations, but a significant drop in insecticide susceptibility of mosquitoes to pyrethroids was observed and the decision was made to switch to a carbamate for the 2011 operations. Insecticide susceptibility to pyrethroids increased after this rotation and remained high in 2012.

Spray operations have been organized by PMI implementing partners under the direction of the NMCP, the Hygiene Service, UCAD, and district health management teams. PMI support includes training and equipping locally-recruited spraying agents with help from the NMCP and its vector control partners, with supervision by the National Hygiene Service. All spray rounds were followed by post-spray evaluation meetings to identify lessons learned and opportunities for improving the next round.

Entomologic Monitoring: During the eight months following the end of the 2014 spray round, entomologists from UCAD, the Parasite Control Service, *Institut Pasteur Dakar*, and IRD conducted entomologic monitoring in five villages in each of the four IRS districts (Koumpentoum, Koungheul, Malem Hodar, and Vélingara) and three and five villages respectively in two neighboring non-IRS districts, Kaffrine and Kolda. The monitoring included cone bioassays on walls to test for insecticidal activity (not in the non-IRS districts), knockdown spray catches, and human landing catches. The mortality results of cone bioassays on bendiocarb-sprayed walls were 100% within the first month of spraying but by the end of the second month had decreased to 52-65%. Thus, as in previous years, the insecticidal activity of bendiocarb appeared to endure no more than two months. The insecticidal effect of pyrimiphos-methyl ranged from 96 to 100% in the first four months of spraying in Koumpentoum but was only 82% in the first two months following spraying in Vélingara but increased to 97% in the third and fourth month. In the fifth month the mortality rates had decreased to 80% in both districts.

Mosquitoes continue to bite indoors as well as outdoors but at lower rates both indoors and outdoors in the IRS districts than in the comparison districts. Data collection was incomplete for Kolda in the month of October and a comparison could not be made for that month. Parity rates varied from month to month in both Vélingara and Kolda, with no clear pattern; therefore no conclusions can be made as to whether the insecticide was having an effect on longevity of the vectors.

Insecticide resistance assays were conducted in 21 geographically dispersed districts of Senegal. Assays were performed with insecticides of all four classes but not all insecticides were tested in all districts. The data showed that vector susceptibility to pyrimiphos-methyl was high throughout the country. Bendiocarb susceptibility remained high (100%) in the two districts where this insecticide was used for IRS but was very low in the region of Dakar (Dakar Center: 9%, Guédiawaye: 64% and Pikine: 34%). Pyrethroid resistance varied greatly whereas DDT resistance was evident in almost all sites.

Spray Operations: In November 2014, the IRS steering committee, composed of representatives from the NMCP, entomologists from UCAD, the National Hygiene Service, the National Directorate of Environment and Agriculture, the IRS implementing partner, and PMI, decided to cease spray operations in Vélingara because this district benefitted from a recent LLIN campaign and the use of SMC and because the entomological and routine health systems data did not provide convincing evidence of a benefit from IRS. The committee decided to return to Nioro where malaria incidence had increased in the past couple of years. A long-lasting organophosphate was chosen for use in the districts of Koumpentoum, Malem Hodar, and Nioro. Because the stock of bendiocarb remaining after the 2014 campaign was almost sufficient to cover Koungheul District, and because this district had a lower malaria incidence than the other IRS districts, the committee decided to maintain bendiocarb for this district.

Preparations for operations in the four districts began in March 2015, including reviewing training tools, preparing soak pits, recruiting seasonal spray operators, and training. This is the first year that "hotspots" will be targeted. Because the activities were limited to the four districts, the steering committee decided to include health post zones with incidences less than 30 per 1,000. Spraying activities began in June in two of the districts treated with pyrimiphos-methyl (Koumpentoum and Nioro), and in Koungheul spraying began in early July to ensure optimal coverage of the transmission season given the short duration of bendiocarb action. Because of the close proximity to Koungheul to decrease the cost of spray operations, the spray activities in the four health post zones of Malem Hodar were carried out at the same time as Koungheul. A total of 111,201 structures were sprayed (out of 114,220 targeted) and 434,201 people were protected (preliminary data as of August 2015). Despite the many challenges involved in IRS implementation, routine monitoring of spray operations suggests that high rates of acceptance have been consistently achieved in all spray rounds.

Plans and justification

With FY 2016 funds, PMI plans to continue spray operations and entomological monitoring in hot spots in selected districts based on the malaria incidence and entomological data. The insecticide chosen for FY 2016 will be a long-acting organophosphate. Together with the NMCP, PMI plans to reassess the IRS strategy once the evaluation of the 2015 focal (hot spot) spraying campaign has been completed.

Proposed activities with FY 2016 funding ($2,944,000)

1. *IRS operations ($2,470,000)*
With FY 2016 funds, PMI plans to support one round of spray operations in malaria hot spots in selected districts with an incidence of malaria between 30 and 50 per 1,000 and based on entomological data. Within these districts, eligible areas include health post zones with an incidence greater than 50 per 1,000 in the previous year and with indoor resting and biting malaria vectors. Number of structures sprayed and people protected will be estimated after districts and health zones have been chosen (approximately 75,000 structures sprayed and 250,000 people protected).

2. *Entomologic monitoring ($400,000)*
PMI plans to continue to support entomologists from UCAD and *Institut Pasteur Dakar* to conduct entomologic M&E for IRS as well as insecticide resistance monitoring (20 sites). Entomologists will conduct cone bioassays at monthly intervals after spraying in selected areas to assess spray quality. Vector behavior will be assessed by monitoring indoor and outdoor biting rates and indoor resting densities. Parity rates will aid in determining female longevity and transmission potential. Finally, mosquito strains will be identified and checked for malaria sporozoites. Baseline entomological data will be collected in malaria hot spots where future IRS activities may take place. Entomologists will continue to conduct insecticide susceptibility assays in the spray districts, the districts where IRS operations have ceased, as well as in additional sites throughout the country where entomologists have been following the evolution of insecticide resistance during the past several years.

3. Technical assistance and supplies for entomologic monitoring ($44,000)
An entomologist from the Centers for Disease Control and Prevention (CDC) will provide technical assistance for the planning and implementation of all PMI-funded entomologic monitoring activities as well as some supplies that have been difficult to obtain through other channels.

4. Environmental monitoring ($30,000)
One visit will be conducted to carry out a required environmental compliance inspection of areas receiving IRS.

3. Malaria in pregnancy

NMCP/PMI objectives

Intermittent preventive treatment in pregnant women with SP given free of charge as directly observed therapy during focused ANC visits was adopted as national policy by the NMCP in 2003 and is implemented in all ANC sites nationwide, regardless of epidemiologic strata. Districts are to purchase SP from the CMS with their health funds for distribution free of charge during ANC visits. The NCMP's Strategic Framework for 2014-2018 articulates that all pregnant women should receive at least three SP doses during their ANC visits, starting in the second trimester and with at least one month between doses. The NMCP's malaria in pregnancy (MIP) objectives are to protect at least 80% of pregnant women with IPTp and for 80% of pregnant women to be protected with an LLIN. In addition, the NMCP aims to treat 100% of pregnant women with confirmed malaria according to national guidelines, using quinine in the first trimester and ACTs in the second and third trimesters. The NMCP's strategy for increasing IPTp uptake includes advocacy for health workers and the population at large, training and supportive supervision of health workers, and outreach activities by health post staff to provide ANC services at the community level at health huts, all of which are supported by PMI.

Progress since PMI was launched

Attendance for ANC is high in Senegal and 97% of pregnant women make at least one visit, with 75% attending three or more visits. However, IPTp coverage remains low with only 40% of pregnant women receiving two doses of SP. PMI has supported the production, dissemination, and use by health care workers of new ANC registers and ANC cards that allow for accurate recording of IPTp treatments, including addition of a third dose of SP; job aids to promote the correct management of malaria in pregnancy and improve the counseling skills of health care providers; water filters/dispensers and re-usable cups for SP administration; and refresher training and supportive supervision. The PMI-supported MIP training is part of integrated malaria training and covers data collection and record-keeping, prevention via IPTp and use of LLINs, and diagnosis and treatment of malaria in pregnant women. PMI supports a routine LLIN distribution system that offers free LLINs to women attending ANC.

Following the WHO recommendation, the NMCP changed its case management policy to allow the treatment of pregnant women diagnosed with uncomplicated malaria during the second and third trimesters with ACTs and maintained the use of quinine during the first trimester. The NMCP has also updated its policy, guidelines, and training manuals to incorporate the WHO recommendation to simplify IPTp guidelines and include the three-dose regimen for IPTp. With PMI's support, updated registers are now being used in health facilities nationwide and include fields to record all three doses of IPTp as well as whether an ITN was provided. The NMCP measures SP dose numbers (1, 2, 3)/first ANC visit (for all women enrolled at their first ANC visit) and for SP (third dose)/first ANC visit the coverage was 35% nationally in 2014, increasing from 14% in 2013

Progress during the last 12-18 months

During the period October 2014-March 2015, 223 facility-based health workers were trained in the prevention, diagnosis, and treatment of malaria in pregnancy. In addition, 20 midwives received training on focused antenatal care (FANC), with an emphasis on IPTp. More than 1,945 outreach visits were made to health huts, resulting in 13,091 prenatal consultations, and 8,204 doses of IPTp distributed.

With PMI's support, approaches to help districts identify and remedy factors decreasing IPTp uptake of SP have been implemented in 13 districts in the regions of Dakar, Diourbel, and Thiès. In Mbour District, for example, IPTp2 coverage increased from 58% to 81% from 2013 to 2014, following implementation of an evidence-based approach. Interviews and focus groups with health care providers, pregnant women, and community members indicated that there was confusion about the policy to provide SP for free, as well as a need to reinforce the IPTp guidelines. This formative research was used to develop key messages that were disseminated through road shows/caravans in the area. In addition, health facility staff were re-trained, cups and water filters were provided to encourage directly-observed administration of SP in facilities, and community members (particularly female leaders who provide health advice to other women in the community) were sensitized on the importance of preventing malaria in pregnant women. The NMCP plans to use a similar approach to improve IPTp2 coverage in other districts during the coming year, first targeting the 13 districts with the lowest IPTp coverage.

Commodity gap analysis

The CMS is expected to procure SP for an anticipated 554,000 pregnant women in 2017, which will cover all SP needs for the country (see Table 6).

Table 6: SP Gap Analysis

Calendar Year	2015	2016	2017
Total Population	13,525,327	13,863,460	14,210,000
SP Needs			
Estimated pregnancies[2]	501,125	513,570	526,300
Total number of pregnant women attending ANC	1,176,325	1,205,538	1,235,420
Total SP Need (in treatments)	1,176,325	1,205,538	1,235,420
Partner Contributions			
SP to be procured by the CMS	1,176,325	1,205,538	1,235,420
Total SP Available			
Total SP Surplus (Gap)	0	0	0

1. Source: Senegal 2013 population census, assuming 2.5% growth per year.
2. Assuming 3.9% of the population becomes pregnant each year and 95% attend at least one ANC visit
3. SP needs calculated assuming that 80% of pregnant women will receive three doses.

Fewer than 7,000 cases of malaria are reported among pregnant women annually and the ACTs needed to treat them are included in the overall ACT gap analysis in the case management section. The CMS also procures quinine for use in severe malaria cases and maintains adequate stocks. Iron/folate supplements (combination pill: 60 mg ferrous sulfate, 250 micrograms folic acid) are provided to pregnant women at ANC visits and are also procured by the CMS.

Plans and justification

With FY 2016 funding, PMI will continue to support activities aimed at reinforcing the provision of effective MIP services in health facilities nationwide. Support will continue for monitoring and supportive supervision of MIP service delivery, improving data collection including IPTp data, and training new staff on MIP. PMI will also continue to encourage collaboration between the NMCP and the Division of Reproductive Health and Child Survival to strengthen and streamline MIP activities.

Proposed activities with FY 2016 funding ($700,000)

1. *Reinforce provision of effective malaria in pregnancy services in health facilities and through outreach strategies ($700,000)*
PMI will support Senegal's efforts to reposition the prevention of malaria in pregnancy. Building on the successful evidence-based methodology in the districts cited above, PMI will support the ongoing scale-up of this approach to additional districts. Support will include training for new health-facility level providers as needed on prevention and treatment of malaria during pregnancy, which includes topics such as the importance of LLIN use in pregnancy, diagnosis and management of MIP, and counseling and interpersonal communication skills. PMI also plans

to continue to provide cups and water filters as needed for directly-observed treatment with SP. Support will continue for ANC outreach activities at health huts. Activities related to LLIN use and BCC are covered in those sections.

4. Case management

a. Diagnosis and Treatment

NMCP/PMI objectives

The NMCP's objectives include:
- ≥ 99% of health facilities have RDTs and ACTs available;
- 100% of suspected cases tested in pre-elimination zones;
- ≥ 95% of suspected cases tested with an RDT in malaria control zones;
- 100% of confirmed cases of malaria treated according to national policy; and
- 100% of children under 10 years with signs of severe malaria receive pre-referral treatment.

The NMCP has adopted WHO recommendations regarding case investigation and active case detection in districts in which annual incidence is less than 5 per 1,000. In those areas, a confirmed malaria case triggers an investigation of the patient's household and neighboring houses. All members of the index case's household are tested and, in neighboring households, anyone who is symptomatic, has traveled recently, or is not using a LLIN is tested. All who test positive receive an ACT, and, beginning in 2016, confirmed cases will also receive low-dose primaquine.

Another active case finding strategy Senegal has implemented is PECADOM Plus, targeted at high transmission districts to reduce morbidity and mortality. This strategy uses DSDOMs to visit every household in their communities once per week during the high transmission season to identify and test fever cases and treat the positives in all age groups. As the DSDOMs are also trained to identify and treat diarrhea and pneumonia in children under five, they screen for this as well during the sweeps.

Progress since PMI was launched

The NMCP adopted ACTs as first-line treatment in 2006 and introduced RDTs in 2007. Both AL and AS-AQ were adopted simultaneously as first-line treatments, with AS-AQ being procured from the beginning, and AL procurement starting in 2010. In addition, dihydroartemisinin-piperaquine donated by the Chinese government is also used in the public health sector and is considered a third first-line treatment. Quinine is used for treatment of severe malaria in all age groups and in pregnant women in the first trimester (with ACTs in the second and third trimesters). Intravenous artesunate was adopted along with quinine as first-line therapy for severe malaria, but this policy is being gradually implemented.

Rapid diagnostic tests were introduced in formal health facilities in late 2007, along with a diagnostic algorithm specifying that if another obvious cause of fever was present, a patient would not be tested with an RDT nor be reported as a suspected malaria case, but be treated for that illness and be eligible to return for re-evaluation, including an RDT, if symptoms persisted. At the community level, RDTs were introduced in 2008, and all fevers are eligible for testing. Positive cases showing no signs of severity are treated with ACTs, while negative and severe cases are referred to the nearest health post.

Senegal recently introduced three WHO recommendations: (1) pre-referral treatment with rectal artesunate for severe malaria, both at the health post level and at the community level; (2) intravenous artesunate as a co-first line for treatment of severe malaria; and (3) SMC with one treatment of SP-AQ monthly during the rainy season. Much of the existing research on SMC was conducted in Senegal, first in children under five, and subsequently in children up to ten years of age. In Senegal, four southern regions (Sédhiou, Kolda, Tambacounda, and Kédougou) meet all the WHO criteria for SMC (at least 60% of cases within four months, at least 10% annual incidence among children).

PMI has supported both diagnosis and treatment of malaria through integrated training of health care providers at all levels, supportive supervision, and commodity procurement. In addition, PMI has provided microscopes, trained laboratory technicians, and supported quality assurance/quality control systems for microscopy. At the community level, PMI supports two different activities: health huts and home-based management of malaria (PECADOM). Health huts, staffed by community health workers (*agents de santé communautaire*), offer an integrated package of maternal and child health interventions, which has included malaria case management with RDTs and ACTs since 2008. PECADOM was piloted in 2008, and scaled up to nearly 1,000 villages by 2010. Under this model, a home-based care provider (*dispensateur de soins à domicile* or DSDOM) is chosen by a community at least 5 kilometers from the nearest health post, and trained in management of malaria with RDTs and ACTs. Diagnosis and treatment are provided to patients of all ages. In 2012, an integrated home-based package (integrated PECADOM), including treatment of diarrhea and pneumonia for children under five years old was piloted among 88 DSDOMs in five districts. Based on the results of this experience, integrated PECADOM is being expanded nationwide.

Progress during the last 12–18 months

Diagnosis: In the last 12 months, PMI supported 343 training and supervision/quality control visits to 118 health facilities; in total 88 technicians (13 regional biologists and 75 district laboratory technicians) were either trained or supervised, covering all public sector laboratories with microscopy capacity. During the quality control visits, the supervisors complete a supervision checklist, verify five negative and five positive slides that the microscopists have read, and have the microscopists read a panel of pre-selected slides. In addition, 77 (65%) of the 118 health facilities have provided the desired number of positive and negative slides for laboratory quality control, 10 positive and 10 negative slides to Dakar for concurrence by the UCAD reference laboratory. For positive slides, 52% of health facilities were classified as having either 'very good' or 'good' levels of competence in slide interpretation, while for negative slides, this rate was 93% for the same levels of proficiency. This evaluation led to the identification of health facilities for remedial training and increased supervision.

In addition, PMI supported the evaluation of quality control of RDTs, selecting 25 RDTs from three different lots upon arrival in Senegal. These were tested against standard reference samples with either 200 or 2,000 parasites per microliter, and also negative controls. All RDTs performed as expected, with 100% sensitivity and 100% specificity. In the next year, PMI partners plan to expand this quality control effort to include collection of tests at different time points from health facilities to evaluate possible changes in test performance related to storage conditions.

The PMI team and partners in Senegal completed data collection for a PMI-funded operational research project to evaluate the diagnostic algorithm, specifically to determine the proportion of patients not tested with an RDT according to the NMCP's diagnostic algorithm who actually have parasitemia. While the sensitivity of the algorithm to identify malaria parasitemia (compared to RDTs) is >80% in most of the country and in patients above the age of five, sensitivity is only 75% in the southeast and only 68% among children under five years. As a result of these findings, the NMCP decided to update the algorithm. Beginning in May 2015, all children under five years of age presenting with fever are expected to be tested for malaria, with subsequent treatment for all confirmed cases. A transitional diagnostic strategy was adopted in early 2015 until universal testing of all patients with fever or a history of fever can be rolled out in 2017. During 2016, all children under five years of age all year round and patients above five years of age with fever during July–January will be tested for malaria. Patients above five years of age from February to June with another evident cause for fever will not be tested for malaria and the suspected cause of illness will be treated. If no improvement is seen in 48 hours, then malaria testing is recommended. Senegal plans to move to universal testing of fever cases in all age groups throughout the year in 2017, once experience in quantification of RDTs is gained and funding for likely extra needed RDTs is secured.

Treatment: PMI procured 800,950 ACT treatments (371,750 AL targeted primarily to SMC regions and 429,200 AS-AQ). Case management activities in the formal health sector included training and supportive supervision, using a strategy of peer supervision and mentoring termed TutoratPlus. During FY 2014, PMI supported the training of 249 health workers at the facility level and 155 at the community level on malaria case management including RDTs and ACTs. Through PMI funding, the NMCP trained 2,733 people on the new case management directives and supervised 1,099 health workers at 86 health centers and 173 health posts.

Implementation of SMC in 2014 covered 16 southeastern districts with three rounds of SMC. A total of 624,139 children under 10 years of age were targeted to receive AS-AQ, and 616,278 (99%) received at least one treatment during the three SMC rounds. PMI procured the drugs and paid for part of the operational costs; UNICEF contributed to cover these costs. PMI worked closely with the NMCP to develop the implementation and monitoring plan. This new intervention is being rigorously monitored and evaluated using routine morbidity and mortality data, pharmacovigilance, monitoring of molecular markers, and process indicators, as recommended by WHO. Currently no other donors have agreed to support the campaign for FY 2016.

For treatment of severe disease, the NMCP introduced pre-referral treatment with rectal artesunate (for children aged 6 months to 6 years) in preparation for the 2014 transmission season. Following official adoption of the policy, national guidelines and manuals were updated. Health post nurses nationwide were trained on drug administration and procedures for referring patients to higher level facilities for the correct treatment of severe disease and stocks were put in place. A community-level pilot is underway in the high-transmission districts of Saraya and Salemata. Senegal has introduced intravenous artesunate at selected hospitals and health centers.

The community-level program now includes a total of 2,162 health huts and 1,992 DSDOMs. At the community level, integrated PECADOM was scaled up to 492 DSDOMs in Tambacounda and Kédougou regions. PECADOM Plus, an active version of PECADOM, was piloted in 15 villages in Saraya District (Kédougou Region), in partnership with Peace Corps and the NMCP in 2013. This strategy uses DSDOMs to visit every household in their communities once per week during 21 weeks of the high transmission season to identify and test fever cases and treat the positives. An additional 15 villages with DSDOMs served as comparison, and household visits were conducted at baseline, midline, and endline in these villages. The point prevalence of symptomatic malaria was 1.1% in both comparison and intervention villages at baseline, but by the final week (three weeks after the first round of SMC), intervention villages had a point prevalence of symptomatic malaria of 0.2%, compared to 2.9% in comparison villages. Based on these favorable results, the NMCP expanded PECADOM Plus as an additional strategy to increase access to care in the high-prevalence regions of Kédougou in 2014 and Kolda in 2015, with plans to further expand to other high-incidence districts in the years to come. In 2014, 132 DSDOMs participated over 21 weeks, identifying and testing 10,131 cases of fever and diagnosing and treating 8,069 cases of malaria.

Commodity gap analysis
While ACT needs for treatment are expected to decrease with the introduction of SMC, RDT needs may not significantly change, and increased use of both through active case detection strategies and expansion of PECADOM may lead to either increased or similar needs. The ACT needs presented here are based on consumption data from recent years, while the RDT analysis takes into account the various case detection and case investigation activities that are planned. The IDB has recently announced that it will provide funding for RDTs. Of note, case management policy change in response to operational research results is likely to significantly increase RDT needs, though it is unclear to what degree, and RDT needs have not yet been re-calculated. PMI plans to assure sufficient RDTs to account for the increase in testing.

Table 7: RDT Gap Analysis

Calendar Year	2015	2016	2017
RDT Needs			
Target population at risk for malaria[1]	14,318,196	14,704,787	15,101,817
Total number projected fever cases[2]	2,500,000	2,500,000	2,500,000
Percent of fever cases confirmed with microscopy	NA	NA	NA
Percent of fever cases confirmed with RDT[3]	78%	87%	99%
Total RDT Needs[4]	**1,929,110**	**2,186,485**	**2,478,198**
Partner Contributions			
RDTs carried over from previous year	NA	NA	313,515
RDTs from MoH	0	0	0
RDTs from Global Fund	0	0	0
RDTs from IDB	NA	1,000,000	0
RDTs planned with PMI funding	1,900,000	1,500,000	2,500,000
Total RDTs Available	**1,900,000**	**2,500,000**	**2,813,515**
Total RDT Surplus (Gap)	**(29,110)**	**313,515**	**335,317**

(1) Population estimates are projections derived from the last census. (2) Total number of fever cases is based on discussions among partners and the percentage of positive testing in Senegal. (3) Percentage of tested fever cases increase on a yearly basis due to the gradual implementation of universal testing for malaria. (4) RDT needs include buffer stocks at the different levels of the health system.

Table 8: ACT Gap Analysis

Calendar Year	2015	2016	2017
ACT Needs			
Target population at risk for malaria[1]	14,318,196	14,704,787	15,101,817
Total projected number of malaria cases	605,593	573,422	542,961
Total ACT Needs[2]	**706,525**	**668,992**	**633,454**
Partner Contributions			
ACTs carried over from previous year	NA	NA	631,008
ACTs from MoH	0	0	0
ACTs from Global Fund	0	0	0
ACTs from IDB	0	700,000	0
ACTs planned with PMI funding	600,000	600,000	800,000
Total ACTs Available	**600,000**	**1,300,000**	**1,431,008**
Total ACT Surplus (Gap)	**(106,525)**	**631,008**	**797,554**

(1) Population estimates are projections derived from the last census. (2) ACT needs include buffer stocks at the different levels of the health system. Total ACT quantities include buffer stocks at different levels of the supply chain system.

Plans and justification

PMI will maintain its support for the diagnosis and treatment activities described above (training, supervision, procurement), for both uncomplicated and severe disease. With the expected increase in the number of districts with very low annual incidence (nearing or less than 5 per 1,000; 14 districts in 2013), the NMCP plans to begin the process of policy change to introduce a single low dose of primaquine in association with ACT treatment for confirmed malaria cases, in accordance with WHO guidelines. Introduction of this approach is planned for selected districts with annual incidence < 5 per 1,000. Research on safety and G6PD deficiency prevalence is currently ongoing to support the introduction in 2016. Finally, PMI will continue to support therapeutic efficacy monitoring in two sites annually, rotating sites.

Proposed activities with FY 2016 funding ($7,533,000)

Diagnosis

1. *Strengthening microscopic diagnosis of malaria ($200,000)*
PMI plans to continue to provide training in microscopic diagnosis of malaria for new microscopists, as well as remedial training for those found not proficient during supervision. PMI plans to provide supportive supervision of malaria diagnosis by microscopy for laboratory and health facility staff and assist the NMCP and its partners to implement the quality assurance and control standards for malaria diagnostic testing. Sites showing poor performance will be targeted for additional on-site training and quality control visits.

2. *Procurement of microscopes and laboratory consumables ($30,000)*
PMI plans to provide laboratory consumables and to replace aging microscopes if needed.

3. *Procurement of RDTs ($1,500,000)*
The NMCP has requested that PMI procure approximately 2.5 million RDTs to contribute to nationwide needs, including diagnosis of symptomatic patients at health facilities, at community level, and active case detection where indicated.

4. *Quality control of microscopy and RDTs ($25,000)*
PMI plans to assist in the implementation of quality control programs for both microscopy and RDTs, in conjunction with NMCP and the Université Cheikh Anta Diop. This includes review of a percentage of positive and negative slides as well as the evaluation of RDTs upon arrival in Senegal and at regular intervals thereafter.

Treatment

1. *Improve case management at health facilities ($500,000)*
As part of the effort to improve the management of malaria, PMI plans to support training for health care workers in case management with RDTs and ACTs (initial and refresher training, as indicated), as well as management of severe disease. Implementing partners will work with the MoH to provide supportive supervision in the correct management of malaria at health posts, health centers, hospitals, and in the private sector.

2. *Strengthen community case management ($500,000)*
With FY 2016 funding, PMI plans to continue to provide technical support on correct diagnosis, treatment, stock management, and referral practices for CHWs at health huts. Attention will also be given to timely data collection and integration of community case management data into the MoH reporting system. The PMI funding will complement other USAID/MCH funding to support the training, supervision, and monitoring of community-based staff.

3. *Intensification of integrated home-based management of malaria (integrated PECADOM) and PECADOM Plus ($1,500,000)*

PMI plans to continue to support supervision of village malaria workers in malaria diagnosis with RDTs and treatment with ACTs as part of an integrated case management package that includes acute respiratory infections and diarrhea, which includes support to health post nurses and DSDOMs. PMI plans to support operational costs to extend integrated PECADOM Plus in the south (Kédougou, Kolda, Tambacounda, and Sédhiou regions), including existing DSDOM and CHWs at health huts and also the expansion to cover more villages in these regions with DSDOMs.

4. *Procure ACTs ($783,000)*

PMI plans to procure approximately 800,000 ACT treatments, which will meet the majority of the country's needs for the year. Artemether-lumefantrine will be procured and distributed in the four regions where SMC is implemented to avoid treating confirmed malaria cases with the same drug that is used for chemoprevention (amodiaquine). In previous years, approximately half of the country's malaria cases have occurred in these regions. Artesunate-amodiaquine will be procured and targeted to the remaining regions.

5. *Operational costs ($1,500,000) and procurement of drugs ($600,000) for implementation of SMC*

PMI plans to continue to fund SMC with three or four doses of SP-AQ for children from three months to ten years in the four highest transmission regions. The age groups and geographic zones may be re-evaluated based on experience. The operational funds are slated to support training, supplies, and supervision. Funds for communications activities are included in the BCC section. The intervention should cover approximately 600,000 children for three months, with the Kédougou Region adding a fourth month to cover a longer transmission season. PMI plans to work with the NMCP and its partners to make sure adequate funds are available to fill any gaps to successfully implement this activity.

6. *Operational costs of expanding pre-referral treatment to the community level nationwide ($150,000), procurement of rectal artesunate suppositories ($40,000), and procurement of injectable artesunate for treatment of severe malaria ($55,000)*

PMI plans to continue to procure 45,000 doses (100mg per dose) of rectal artesunate for pre-referral treatment for severe malaria. Pre-referral treatment with rectal artesunate at the community level will be scaled up nationwide. The budget/quantity for procurement of rectal artesunate will be revised as necessary. PMI plans to procure approximately 21,000 treatments (5 ampules per treatment) of injectable artesunate sufficient to treat cases of severe malaria referred to the hospital or health center level. While the expectation is that the number of severe cases will decrease, this amount is sufficient to meet approximately 30% of the need, if the incidence of severe malaria does not decrease from 2013 levels.

7. *Procurement of primaquine ($10,000) and implementation of single low-dose primaquine in elimination districts ($40,000)*

PMI plans to procure primaquine for single low-dose treatment in elimination districts with incidence approximately 1 per 1,000. PMI will target the region of Saint-Louis and Louga, which has five health districts, a population of approximately 980,000, and a malaria incidence of 1.6

per 1,000. PMI will also support a detailed M&E plan, which will likely include regular supervision, data analysis, case investigation, and pharmacovigilance. Operational funds will cover training, job aids, and supervision.

8. *Therapeutic efficacy monitoring ($100,000)*
PMI plans to support therapeutic efficacy studies at two sites to monitor the susceptibility of *P. falciparum* to the first-line ACTs (artesunate-amodiaquine and artemether-lumefantrine) and monitor molecular resistance markers for SP, amodiaquine, and artesunate. Sites for therapeutic efficacy studies will be rotated to provide data from western, central, and southeastern Senegal. Four sites are rotated: Deggo (Dakar), Keur Soce (Central), and two in the South (Velingara and Kedougou). Both southern sites are areas with a great deal of regional population movement, with the Kedougou site also known for a great influx associated with mining. PMI plans to conduct TES in two sites annually, testing the three ACTs in circulation in Senegal each year. A UCAD laboratory has developed advanced molecular capacity to test for K13. This laboratory has the capacity to become a regional testing center, and we plan to conduct K13 testing in Senegal to build capacity and avoid ethical issues associated with exporting samples. Data from the first year of testing are now available; there is still 100% PCR-corrected ACPR at 28 and 42 days to all three ACTs (results available for Dakar only).

b. Pharmaceutical Management

NMCP/PMI objectives

The ultimate goal of PMI's support for the supply chain is to ensure that SP, ACTs, and RDTs are procured and made available in sufficient quantities at all service delivery points. In its strategic plan, the NMCP's specific objective for pharmaceutical management is to ensure the availability of antimalarial drugs and products in at least 95 percent of all public and community facilities.

Progress since PMI was launched

To address recurrent stockouts of several commodities, in 2011 PMI supported an assessment of the CMS aimed at identifying root problems and potential solutions. Challenges identified by the assessment included the lack of a procedures manual, inadequate utilization of the commodity management information system, and insufficient capacity among various personnel. PMI then provided assistance to update the procedures manual, which was disseminated throughout the health system to chief pharmacists, accountants, and other staff. Also, a new drug management software (SAGE) was developed and installed at the CMS. Technical assistance from PMI has also supported efforts to improve stock management at the lowest levels of the system, with an emphasis on ensuring good ACT prescribing and dispensing practices at health posts and health huts.

Progress during the last 12-18 months

PMI continued its support to the CMS by providing technical assistance to develop a strategic plan for 2014-2018 that will guide it towards meeting the challenges it is facing, with all stakeholders sharing the same vision. Some specific improvements have been made and new initiatives are being piloted, including a mobile pharmacy for the three regions that do not have a pharmacy structure, and the Informed Push Model for some essential products (including malaria in one region). In May 2015, with PMI funding, the first integrated and evaluative supervision visits were conducted by the NMCP and the Department of Reproductive Health and Child Survival in seven health facilities in Joal (Thiès Region) using end-use verification tools. The preliminary findings show that the availability of essential drugs (including ACTs, RDTs and SP) is still weak in health facilities. None of the health facilities visited had ACTs in stock and 43% had expired drugs in storage. In addition, 57% of health facilities reported that they do not order drugs on a regular basis and 14% of drug managers had not received training in the past three years. Efforts will continue to increase supervision to make ACTs available on a permanent basis at all health facilities.

Following the development of its 2014-2018 strategic plan, the CMS designed a project with the aim of improving drug distribution from regional pharmacies to health districts to increase availability in health facilities (health centers and health posts). Known as "*Jegessi naa*" ("we are getting closer" in the Wolof language), the project started in January 2015 and is being piloted in three districts. Although it is too premature to assess the impact of the project on health care delivery, anecdotal reports from the field, mainly from Fatick Medical Region, indicate that availability of essential drugs at health post depots has improved. The Mission will use PMI and other health element resources to support the evaluation of the project one year into implementation in order to learn lessons and support scale-up as necessary.

In FY 2014 PMI continued its support to activities aimed at improving governance of the health system for increased access and quality service delivery. Under the leadership of the MoH, Senegal has been piloting Performance-Based Financing (PBF) in three districts. After one year of implementation, an evaluation of the pilot demonstrated that PMI-supported activities, including training and supervision in three districts, contributed to improving those malaria prevention and case management services for which compensation is paid. Because IPTp coverage is an indicator included in the PBF management plan and is compensated, the uptake of IPTp has significantly increased in the target districts. In the District of Kaffrine for example, IPTp coverage has improved from 29% to 48% over a one-year period and from 31% to 69% in the District of Birkelane. Moreover, SP stockouts have been reduced considerably due to appropriate steps taken by service providers to ensure SP availability on a permanent basis during ANC services. Discussions are underway between USAID, the MoH, and the World Bank to expand the number of districts covered by PBF, which will contribute to the Government of Senegal's vision of Universal Health Coverage.

Plans and justification

Under its next 2015-2021 health strategy, the Mission plans on enhancing its support to the supply chain and pharmaceutical system. The resources of the current MOP will coincide with the first year of the strategy. Therefore, PMI resources together will other program element funding will contribute to implement mission's support to improve the performance of the CMS and make commodities available at service delivery points.

Proposed activities with FY 2016 funding ($1,025,000)

With FY 2016 funding, PMI plans to support the following activities to strengthen the health system and develop capacity at sub-national and central levels.

1. Support supply chain management at the central level ($800,000)
With FY 2016 funds, PMI plans to continue to support the implementation of key reforms instituted during prior years and provide technical assistance to improve drugs and RDTs quantification through the use of consumption data collected from peripheral levels.

2.   Drug quality monitoring and advocacy ($225,000)
In collaboration with the NMCP, the Directorate of Pharmacies and Medicines and the National Drug Control Laboratory, PMI plans to continue its support to drug quality monitoring activities in nine sites. In addition, PMI plans to support advocacy for policy enforcement of drug quality standards. Proposed activities will also include technical assistance to the National Drug Control Laboratory as it seeks to meet the requirements to be a regional reference laboratory.

5. Health system strengthening and capacity building

PMI supports a broad array of health system strengthening activities which cut across intervention areas, such as training of health workers, supply chain management and health information systems strengthening, drug quality monitoring, and NCMP capacity building.

NMCP/PMI objectives

The 2011 – 2015 National Strategic Plan identifies three key objectives for health system strengthening:
  1. Ensure the availability of antimalarial drugs and products in at least 95 percent of all public and community facilities.
  2. Strengthen the managerial and operational capabilities of health personnel at all levels of the health system.
  3. Ensure the timeliness, completeness and use of data for M&E of the 2011-2015 National Strategic Plan.

These objectives have been carried over into the new 2014-2018 Strategic Framework. Major partners currently supporting the health system in Senegal are France Development Agency, the African Development Bank, the World Bank, the Belgium Technical Cooperation, the Spanish Cooperation, AMREF, JICA, the GFATM-Health System Strengthening, GAVI-HSS, the Luxembourg Development Agency, UNFPA, and USAID. The CMS is pivotal to the health system and is mandated to make essential drugs accessible to the population in a timely manner.

Progress since PMI was launched

Since beginning work in Senegal, PMI has supported health system strengthening and capacity building of the MoH to implement its malaria control program. Specific interventions include pharmaceutical management activities, training, supervision, drug quality monitoring, and policy reform. In 2014, and to comply with the Global Fund New Funding Model requirements, the NMCP conducted a review of the program's performance that led to the development of the concept note submitted to the Global Fund. Basically, the program's objectives were maintained with the malaria pre-elimination objective by 2018.

PMI has reinforced its efforts to build capacity and integrate across programs. PMI has supported the CMS through the mobile distribution, a push system that is being experimented and consolidated by the Government of Senegal to achieve its health objectives. Training was provided to pharmacy managers on supply chain management as part of an integrated activity covering principles that apply to all essential drugs. Similarly, malaria drug quality monitoring was integrated with medicines for the treatment of tuberculosis and HIV/AIDS, as well as oral contraceptives, with different programs contributing to support the overall budget.

Capacity building: For the past several years, PMI has supported the NMCP to supervise case management at hospitals, health centers, and health posts. PMI helps build national capacity in malaria control by supporting an annual malariology course and in M&E through funding the attendance of health system staff at the annual data management and M&E course at the African Center for Advanced Management Studies (*Centre Africain des Etudes Supérieures en Gestion*). In 2012, PMI was closely involved in developing and shepherding through policy changes related to case management and prevention.

Progress during the last 12-18 months

As in the past four years, PMI's support to the health system during the past 12 to 18 months covered three main areas: a) support to the CMS, b) support to the on-going results-based financing activities, and c) support to the NMCP institutional capacity strengthening.
PMI resources contribute to the Performance-Based Financing (PBF) since its experimentation started in Senegal in 2012. PBF was put in place in 4 southern regions (Ziguinchor, Sedhiou, Tambacounda, and Kedougou) with high malaria prevalence and low coverage indicators in 2013. The malaria indicators are the number of pregnant women who received two doses of IPTp and the number of cases of uncomplicated malaria that received correct treatment. The overall cases decreased from 10,891 in 2013 to 6,641 and the proportion receiving correct treatment remained over 95%. While the number of posts included in the program only increased from 102 to 110, the number of pregnant women who received two or more doses of IPTp increased from 19,746 to 33,751, an increase of 71%. Stockouts continue to be reduced under the PBF scheme as health managers and care providers take all appropriate actions to make SP, RDTs and ACTs available for IPTp and case management services. Expansion of the PBF activities is scheduled to start in 2015 with financial support from the World Bank.

Capacity building: Integrated logistics supervision visits were conducted at all regional medical stores and health districts, and PMI also supported the NMCP to supervise case management at hospitals, health centers, and health posts. Upon the NMCP's request and following the organizational audit conducted in 2013, a detailed report was delivered highlighting the weaknesses, the strengths and the opportunities that the NMCP present. Most of the areas identified for improvement include governance, training, management and partnership.

Plans and justification

The NMCP requires ongoing skills development to respond to changes in malaria trends. Increased supervision is also necessary at all levels of the health system to ensure that policies and guidelines are implemented as appropriate. Besides concentrating on improving data collection to monitor drug availability and distribution, drug quality control activities will continue to receive more attention. With FY 2016 funding, PMI plans to support activities to develop capacity at sub-national and central levels to continue working towards the attainment of the NMCP's pre-elimination objective. More concretely, PMI will complement other Mission health programs to promote local governance by strengthening the capacity of local elected officials to address malaria as a priority in local development plans and increasing participation of communities in decision-making and financing. Also, PMI will encourage the NMCP to empower their staff at the decentralized level to plan, manage and coordinate activities and allocate resources as appropriate to achieve expected results. As the government of Senegal deems appropriate pursuing the PBF experiment, PMI will work with the World Bank and other interested donors to expand the reach of the program and contribute to better impact on malaria prevention and control.

Peace Corps: Active linkages with Peace Corps volunteers are planned to continue, allowing volunteers and their communities to benefit from the technical resources that partners provide. In this partnership, PMI benefits from the committed community presence of more than 200 volunteers, making it the largest Peace Corps program in the world. While malaria funds have not in the past supported the third year malaria coordinator, they will in the future. Specific projects that require funding will be submitted to the Small Project Assistance committee for approval. Projects that have been funded in the past include net care and repair activities, piloting the active detection of fever cases, training women's groups/community care groups, and organizing malaria fairs.

Proposed activities with FY 2016 funding ($755,000)

(1) NMCP capacity building

- *Support to NMCP to enable program supervision ($250,000)*
  With FY 2016 funds, PMI plans to contribute to the NMCP's supportive supervision visits to regional and health district levels. Supervision at health posts, health centers, and hospitals will continue to receive increased attention.

- *State of the art capacity building opportunities ($30,000)*
  With the objective of achieving malaria pre-elimination by 2018, NMCP personnel and the country program will greatly benefit from participating in international technical, scientific, and professional meetings that present opportunities to learn best practices, share experiences, and develop networks. Potential meetings include the American Society for Tropical Medicine and Hygiene and the Pan-African Malaria Conference. PMI would encourage the NMCP to seek funding from the MoH and conference organizers before supporting participation at such events.

- *Malariology course ($100,000)*
  The NMCP is requesting PMI's support for the creation of a malariology course (including curriculum development) that would be offered to health staff at various levels and would allow for in-country training opportunities. This course was developed in 2008, in order to have a trained DHMT leadership that could lead implementation of malaria interventions. PMI has supported it for the past four years. The district leadership turns over regularly, and policies evolve, necessitating continuous availability of the course. The personnel trained in this course are the forefront of implementation, and assure quality supervision. It is offered in conjunction with ISED (the school of public health in Senegal).

(2) Peace Corps

- *Support for specific malaria-related Peace Corps volunteer projects ($25,000)*
  Funds will support a third year volunteer and one or more short term response volunteers as requested by the NMCP, as well as small projects.

(3) Other

- *Support for Performance-Based Financing for malaria indicators ($150,000)*
  A few malaria indicators were selected as part of the PBF performance management plan. PMI plans on providing continued support for the PBF program in participating districts, including training, supervision, data collection and verification, and payment of performance bonuses.

- *Improve governance of local health committees ($200,000)*
  Activities will include supporting the local government to include malaria and other health priorities in their local development plans and increasing participation of communities in decision making regarding health issues. Some planned activities include developing information sharing processes and procedures (e.g., workplans, participatory budgeting, periodic performance and review reporting, radio programming) as well as sensitizing local government entities about the important role that civil society can play in advocating for quality services.

Table 9: Health Systems Strengthening Activities

HSS Building Block	Technical Area	Description of Activity
Health Services	Case Management	PMI will continue supporting training and supervision of health workers in case management in health facilities as well as in health huts and households.
Health Workforce	Health Systems Strengthening	PMI will contribute with other health funding streams to train newly recruited health work force staff as the Government of Senegal engages in filling the human resources gap in the health system to achieve universal coverage of health services.
Health Information	Monitoring and Evaluation	PMI will continue supporting the strengthening of routine information system as well as continuous DHS and DHIS2.
Essential Medical Products, Vaccines, and Technologies	Case Management	PMI will continue supporting the supply chain and drug distribution system through reinforcing the management of the CMS and strengthening the capacity of human resources at the regional level. Activities will include drugs quality control and ensuring quality diagnostic and efficacy of treatment drugs.
Health Finance	Health Systems Strengthening	PMI will work with other partners such as the World Bank and the Global Fund to expand the PBF activities to increase access to malaria prevention measures and case management services.
Leadership and Governance	Health Systems Strengthening	PMI will support activities that strengthen the leadership of the NMCP at each level of the health system as well as encouraging local elected officials and communities to prioritize malaria and other health issues in their local development plans.

6. Behavior change communication

NMCP/PMI objectives

Senegal's current national strategy for malaria communication includes the following objectives:
- Increase the proportion of people sleeping under ITNs to > 80%
- Increase the proportion of pregnant women who take two doses of SP under directly observed treatment at ANC to > 80%
- Increase the proportion of people who seek care at health facilities within 24 hours of the onset of fever to > 80%
- Increase compliance in the treatment of uncomplicated malaria
- Increase acceptance of IRS to > 90% of households in targeted districts (Note: This objective has been achieved in all spray rounds supported by PMI)
- Strengthen partnerships with the private sector, media, local government, Parliament, and other government departments
- Monitor and evaluate the NMCP communication plan

While originally developed to support the goals and objectives of the 2011-2015 National Strategic Plan, the communications strategy remains consistent with the NMCP's 2014-2018 Strategic Framework. The latter emphasizes that IEC/BCC approaches in Senegal should be evidence-based and tailored to specific populations and geographic areas. The NCMP is keen to ensure that approaches are grounded in formative research that identifies key determinants of behavior for specific audiences, appropriate communication channels, and suitable printed materials.

Communications about malaria are expected to take into account local specificities such as differences in net use culture. Since the NMCP implements various malaria control interventions depending on the malaria burden of specific areas (e.g., SMC in four regions, IRS in hotspots of selected districts, etc.) communications efforts are also tailored accordingly. The 2014-2018 Strategic Framework also articulates the NMCP's desire to revitalize the partnership around BCC for malaria so that it encompasses the private sector, community-based organizations, and other sectors of the government. In particular, the NMCP foresees working more closely with primary and elementary schools by providing training for teachers as well as educational tools about malaria prevention and control for students.

Progress since PMI was launched

PMI has supported various community mobilization and BCC activities in Senegal. These include both ongoing malaria communications (mass and interpersonal) and communication activities promoting specific events, such as IRS or LLIN distribution campaigns. Typical communications activities in Senegal have included community meetings on a specific topic, home visits, theater, community radio (radio spots as well as interviews and programming), and social mobilization (setting aside a day to focus on a specific theme or topic and bringing the whole community together around that topic – for speeches, music, skits, with banners and t-shirts with messages, etc.). Topics of ongoing IEC/BCC at community level include the importance of owning and using ITNs, prompt care-seeking in the case of fever, recognition of danger signs, the importance of attending ANC visits, and the importance of receiving the recommended doses of IPTp. Through Peace Corps volunteers and bilateral implementing partners, PMI has supported malaria education and prevention throughout the country.

To date, there has been little if any effort to evaluate the impact of the different communications activities on health/malaria indicators, such as LLIN use or care-seeking behavior. This weakness was expressed often as USAID/Senegal was developing its 2011-2016 health strategy and directly led to the creation of a new program to concentrate on streamlining and "upgrading" communications interventions. Going forward, the focus will be on strategic activities with specific objectives, the results of which can and will be evaluated.

In 2012, the NMCP and National Health Education and Information Service (SNEIPS) created a national Malaria IEC/BCC Coordination Committee to promote harmonization of approaches and activities among the numerous partners. This was followed by a workshop to share actual materials and work plans, and to revise the 2011 malaria BCC plan. PMI supported both of these activities and has taken a lead on ensuring rigor in the development of BCC activities. A team from Senegal, composed of the NMCP, SNEIPS, PMI, and two implementing partners, attended the PMI Malaria BCC workshop in September, 2013. This provided a good opportunity to share perspectives and experience and develop a common plan for moving forward with more evidence-based communications activities. Given the reduction in malaria burden that has been observed in Senegal and the roll out of specific interventions tailored to different parts of the country based on malaria burden, one complexity of the Senegal program is that communications activities need to be tailored to local contexts to reflect the interventions being implemented.

Progress during the last 12-18 months

With PMI's assistance, the NMCP is taking a more strategic and evidence-based approach to developing and implementing communications campaigns, which is described in the NMCP's 2014-2018 Strategic Framework. The NMCP's approach includes identifying the determinants of behaviors related to malaria and using the findings to develop communication campaigns with an appropriate mix of messages and channels. Developed with the technical assistance of professional media/marketing firms and based on the determinants of the behaviors PMI seeks to influence, the new messages speak more directly to the targeted populations. This evidence-based approach will allow PMI to more rigorously gauge the impact of the supported BCC campaigns.

BCC for LLINs:
Social marketing of ITNs: Since 2013, PMI has also supported the implementation of a communications campaign to accompany the introduction of subsidized LLINs in the private sector in large urban areas nationwide. The campaign focuses on increasing brand recognition and creating demand through television and radio spots as well as printed media. Building on the results of market research showing that, for many people, nuisance avoidance is a more important factor for net use than malaria prevention, the campaign emphasizes getting a good night's sleep, the protective qualities of the nets ("MILDA: The mosquito net that kills mosquitoes"), their affordability ("1,000 FCFA for 1,000 nights"), and where to obtain them (pharmacies, grocery stores, gas stations). For this campaign, TV and radio spots were produced and broadcast in major urban areas. Newspaper insertions and internet banners were also used to reach a wide audience. As a result, a total of 189,454 MILDA-branded ITNs were sold over the period 2013 through March 2015. An evaluation of the MILDA social marketing campaign is planned for late 2015.

Mass ITN communications campaign: PMI continued to provide support for the NMCP's overarching communications campaign to increase use of ITNs in general. The campaign, called the "Three Alls" (*Les Trois Toutes: Toute la famille, Toutes les nuits, Toute l'année*) emphasizes that nets must be used by "all the family, all year long, on all nights." The campaign combines mass media and inter-personal communication strategies, all which have been supported with PMI funding. These include the creation of TV spots which have been broadcast on multiple national networks, as well as radio spots and radio shows, and erecting billboards in five major cities. Over the period September 2014-March 2015, with PMI's support, 8,827 radio spots and 35 radio shows were broadcast via community radios. In addition, PMI worked with community-based organizations to sensitize communities (e.g. using road shows) about the importance of using nets; these efforts reached 4,800 people.

An evaluation of the "*Trois Toutes*" campaign began in July 2014 and showed that while the percentage of people who had been exposed to the campaign was fairly high (68%), the majority (62%) could not recall the campaign slogan.

In July 2014, a nationwide population-based survey was conducted to gather more information on the determinants of behavior related to ITN acquisition and use, as well as preferred and most effective communication channels. The survey showed that, while the majority of respondents cite ITN use as a malaria prevention measure (62%), misconceptions about malaria prevention continue to prevail. For example, 49% cite "maintaining a clean home" as one malaria prevention method, 12% cite "drinking clean water," and 12% mention "avoiding exposure to sunlight." While ITN availability both within the public and private sector has improved in Senegal, the perceived high cost of ITNs continues to be a limiting factor in increasing ITN ownership. Among respondents who did not own a net, the top three reasons given were: "I am waiting for the free nationwide ITN distribution campaign" (44%), "ITNs are too expensive" (37%), and "I don't know where to find an ITN" (19%). Urban and rural residents reported different preferences with regards to communication channels, with urban residents preferring television (66%), and rural residents citing community leaders (77%) and radio (76%) as the two top sources.

BCC for IRS: During the 2014 and 2015 spray rounds, PMI continued to support communication activities in areas targeted for IRS to inform beneficiaries about the timing of spray activities, what they can expect, the precautions they need to take (e.g. removing household items before spraying), and the health benefits of IRS. For the 2015 campaign, materials to support BCC activities (posters, training guides, and manuals) were produced to support the NMCP's transition from blanket spraying to focal spraying of hotspots only. NCMP staff met with the communication focal points in areas targeted for the 2015 spray campaign and designed a communications strategy that was adapted to the new hotspots approach. Acceptance of IRS activities since PMI began spraying in Senegal has been high (>90% during each spray round).

BCC for SMC: PMI funded the development of informational materials for the first SMC campaign in four districts in 2013, and UNICEF supported dissemination costs. Materials were reviewed and revised based on that initial experience for the 2014 campaign that was implemented in four regions and these materials will again be used for the 2015 campaign. Acceptance of SMC campaigns has been high, indicating that the population understands the utility of the interventions.

General Malaria BCC: Senegal has a large Peace Corps presence; of the more than 200 volunteers in-country, at least one third conduct malaria-related activities. Peace Corps volunteers continued to play a significant role in disseminating net transformation techniques to communities and training people on net care and repair. Volunteers also hosted local language radio programs, helped test new communications materials, and organized home visits that touch on various malaria themes. For example, during the period October 2014-March 2015, Peace Corps volunteers assisted with the translation of an *aide-memoire* on the dosing regimen for ACTs into three languages for use by community health workers. Other BCC-related activities included hosting 9 malaria radio shows in four languages, training 144 community mobilizers in malaria BCC, and reaching nearly 4,000 community members with outreach activities about malaria prevention and care-seeking.

Similar interpersonal communications activities were implemented through the outreach workers at health huts and sites under USAID's community health program, which covers all 14 regions of the country. During the period October 2014 to March 2015, IEC/BCC activities were carried out in 2,303 health huts and 1,669 community-level sites on a variety of topics such as ITN use and maintenance, signs and symptoms of malaria, early care-seeking, and IPTp. Approximately 7,000 community-level health workers were mobilized to conduct outreach and a total of 933,137 people were reached with malaria IEC/BCC messages during this period. Activities included a variety of interpersonal communication approaches such as home visits, support groups for pregnant women, outreach to grandmothers, care groups, etc.

Since the current communications strategy ends in 2015, the NMCP is preparing a new strategy which will cover the period 2015-2020 to align with the new National Strategic Plan for 2015-2020. To ensure that the revised strategy is evidence-based, the NMCP has requested that formative research be conducted. A study is currently underway, with funding from the Global Fund. As Senegal moves towards the pre-elimination of malaria, a key challenge for communication will be ensuring that populations continue to use malaria prevention tools and seek treatment, even as malaria becomes rarer.

Plans and justification

With FY 2016 funds, PMI will continue to support a range of communications activities to improve the adoption of key malaria prevention and care-seeking behaviors (e.g., net ownership, proper net use, net repair, IPTp, when and where to seek care). The implementation of a universal coverage LLIN campaign in 2016 will be accompanied by intensive communication efforts to encourage the population to obtain and use nets. The NMCP has indicated that the emphasis will be on maintaining high net ownership via the routine distribution systems (ANC, EPI and schools) in 2017. With FY 2016 funds, PMI therefore plans to fund communication efforts that encourage the population to obtain nets through these routine channels – as no campaigns are currently planned for 2017 and beyond. In addition, communication efforts will also encourage other key behaviors, such as prompt care seeking, which is becoming even more important as transmission intensity and acquired immunity decrease. Given that IPTp2 coverage has remained nearly stable at around 40% for the past few years, communications activities planned for 2017 will continue to reinforce messages on the need for pregnant women to obtain at least three doses of SP during their pregnancy.

PMI plans to continue to work in close partnership with the SNEIPS, NMCP, the MoH and other ministries (the Ministry of Education, Ministry of the Family, etc.), private sector entities, and various other local partners. Approaches will maximize the use of effective materials/tools and media products already developed and used successfully in Senegal while also seeking to develop innovative methods. Focused on evidence-based social marketing principles, PMI plans to use a mix of channels to deliver messages that promote malaria-related products and behaviors to targeted populations. Social mobilization and mass media activities will be conducted to reach large numbers of people, while interpersonal communications will be used at the community and health facility levels to reinforce messages and tailor them to individual contexts.

Through participation in the national Malaria IEC/BCC Coordination Committee, PMI plans to continue to promote coordination across ministries, donors, implementing partners, and the private sector to harmonize the implementation of BCC programming. All planned BCC activities will be monitored in order to improve their outcomes and impact.

Proposed activities with FY 2016 funding ($1,100,000)

1. *Development, implementation, and evaluation of BCC activities ($800,000)*
   PMI plans to continue to support the NMCP's strategy to promote appropriate malaria prevention and care-seeking behaviors. This will include ensuring harmonization amongst the PMI-funded partners who work at different levels of the system, from the community level to the central level at the Ministry of Health. These funds will be used for formative research on determinants of behavior (quantitative and qualitative, as indicated), to contract with marketing firms to design materials and campaigns, to fund actual implementation (printing, mass media, national and regional events), and to evaluate results. Some of the campaigns will include messages that can be disseminated nationwide (such as promoting IPTp) while others will be tailored to specific contexts and developed to support particular interventions in localized areas. PMI will also continue working with the NMCP to engage the private sector in malaria prevention efforts as well as primary and elementary schools. PMI's support for the Malaria IEC/BCC Committee (jointly coordinated by the NMCP and SNEIPS) will continue to ensure that communications about malaria are of high quality and have a strong impact.

2. *Community sensitization and mobilization for IRS ($100,000)*
   In light of the change from district-wide spraying to focal spraying of hotspots within districts starting in May 2015, it is particularly important to ensure that populations in areas targeted for IRS are appropriately informed before each spray round. Based on lessons learned from the spray rounds implemented during 2015 and 2016 (focal spraying of hotspots only), FY 2016 funding from PMI will support a variety of sensitization approaches to ensure continued high acceptance rates of IRS during the 2017 campaign. This will include radio spots, community meetings, and house-to-house visits. Information pamphlets and other printed materials for the household visits and social mobilization activities will be updated, printed, and distributed.

3. *Community sensitization and mobilization for SMC ($100,000)*
   In the four regions where SMC is being implemented, PMI will fund the implementation of communications activities to ensure that populations are well-informed of the SMC campaign and acceptance rates continue to be high. Experiences and lessons learned from the previous SMC campaigns (implemented annually with PMI support since 2013) will be utilized to revise and adapt materials as needed. With FY 2016 funds, PMI plans to continue to support the roll-out of the 2017 SMC campaign using a combination of approaches to sensitize communities, including radio spots, community meetings, and house-to-house visits. One potential challenge with communication around SMC is that medicines need to be

given to children who are not ill. The success of the campaign therefore hinges upon gaining the consent of parents/caregivers. PMI therefore particularly emphasizes interpersonal communications to explain the rationale for SMC and the importance of administering all doses. The success of SMC campaign hinges upon the willingness of parents/caregivers to provide preventive treatment to their child even though the child is well and has no symptoms and to continue to administer the two subsequent doses of amodiaquine.

4. *Promotion of LLIN use ($100,000)*
   While private pharmacies/shops/gas stations do have their own commodity distribution systems, these additional PMI funds are needed to cover operational expenses associated with the social marketing of LLINs in the private sector, including packaging (such as providing bar code and logo stickers), transportation from the warehouse to wholesalers, and medical detailers who visit pharmacies to check on stock levels and placement.

7. Monitoring and evaluation

The NMCP objective for M&E is to ensure prompt and complete routine reporting and use of data for M&E of the 2014-2018 Strategic Framework. The approach includes the expansion and strengthening of surveillance sites and intensifying case detection targeted to reaching pre-elimination in 2018.

Progress since PMI was launched

Senegal is known for its robust routine malaria information system, providing prompt and complete data to guide and measure scale-up of malaria control activities. The NMCP gathers routine malaria mortality and morbidity data that is collected by all health posts and sent to health districts on a monthly basis. In this Excel-based system, all relevant malaria data flow up from the community level health huts and DSDOMs through hardcopy register workbooks to health posts, which are then synthesized in Excel forms and sent to the districts. From the districts, data are then sent simultaneously to the regional and central levels. The NMCP also organizes quarterly review meetings with health districts to share malaria burden data as well as policy and technical information. This routine malaria information system was adversely impacted by a nationwide data retention strike in public health facilities from June 2010 to March 2013. The quarterly review meetings resumed in July 2013. In 2014, efforts to backfill missing data was completed and by early 2015, the system was at 94% reporting completeness with data retention still reported to be an issue in a few districts. While there are continued efforts to include private facilities and send their data to the districts, participation remains limited due to concerns with disclosing patient numbers. By early 2015, the MoH supported the development of the District Health Information System (DHIS2) platform for their nationwide, integrated health information system. For malaria, the NMCP M&E director has been actively engaged in the development and roll-out of the DHIS2 and has incorporated all of the malaria indicators currently collected through the Excel workbooks that are used for the routine malaria information system. Currently, the integrated system is reporting at 70% completeness while the malaria system is reporting at 95% and above. The NMCP and the Division of Health Statistics are currently in discussions about improving their partnership and working towards complete adoption by the NMCP of the DHIS2 platform.

Multiple national-level household surveys have been conducted to provide information on key malaria indicators, including MISs in 2006 and 2008, and DHSs in 2005 and 2010, and a post-campaign survey in 2009 to assess the ownership and use of ITNs after a campaign targeting children under five years of age. In 2012-2013, Senegal began implementing a Continuous Demographic Health Survey (cDHS) consisting of population-based and service provision assessment (SPA) components, which provides information to guide programming on a regular basis. The cDHS provides annual estimates of all standard household-level malaria indicators (including anemia and parasitemia) as well as information on the availability and quality of services in the health sector (including private providers). Results are available nationally and by urban/rural and epidemiologic strata annually, and by region every two years. The final report for the 2014-2015 cDHS was disseminated in March 2015. At the time of dissemination, a database was being created to combine the first and second round of cDHS to tabulate regional estimates. The cDHS is supported by USAID, using malaria and other funds, as well as other partners including the MoH, the World Bank, and UNFPA. The Senegalese government has now become a funding partner to the cDHS and is very interested in continuing this survey in Senegal. The cDHS has been adopted among the official annual surveys supported by the government.

A system of epidemic surveillance sites has been operational since 2008, starting in the Senegal River Valley. Ten districts across seven regions (Saint-Louis, Matam, Louga, Kaolack, Dakar, Tambacounda, Kédougou) are now enrolled in the program, each with two sites reporting morbidity, mortality, and stock information on a weekly basis. Beginning in 2012, in the northern region of Saint-Louis, MACEPA initiated a project in the Richard Toll District, where malaria incidence is under 2 per 1,000. All positive patients identified through health facilities are investigated and reactive case detection is conducted in the household and the five closest households of the index case. Based on analysis of data collected during the first two years of the project, MACEPA recommended testing all household members of the index case, and among the five closest households within a 100 meter radius, only testing individuals who are: 1) symptomatic, 2) have traveled recently, or 3) do not sleep under an ITN.

In the four high transmission regions of southeastern Senegal—Tambacounda, Kédougou, Kolda, and Sédhiou—where SMC is implemented, standard M&E protocols and tools as outlined by the WHO SMC Field Manual are used to monitor SMC indicators, molecular markers of resistance to SP and AQ, estimate coverage rates, and assess adherence, and track pharmacovigilance. The routine information collected weekly by the NMCP from the surveillance sites was examined in 2013 and 2014 to determine the impact of SMC on morbidity and mortality. The morbidity data between the surveillance sites and the routine health system were consistent and showed substantial decreases across the key indicators that were being monitored (confirmed malaria cases, hospitalized malaria cases, and number of deaths due to confirmed malaria). Based on the results, the NMCP decided to continue SMC in 2015 and 2016. Entomological monitoring of IRS districts and select non-IRS sites has guided the implementation of targeted IRS activities, and PMI continues to support therapeutic efficacy testing and drug quality monitoring. Table 10 below summarizes the different data collection activities that have been supported by PMI and other partners.

Progress during the last 12-18 months

The 20 epidemic surveillance sites continued to send data on a weekly basis with 100% completeness and prompt reporting. Since March 2013, the NMCP has continued to send out weekly surveillance bulletins to a large and varied group of stakeholders that presents user-friendly data describing trends in malaria burden and commodity availability at each site. With the expansion of reactive case detection activities in three additional districts (Podor, Dagana, Pete) in the Saint-Louis Region, covering four out of five districts in the region, PMI continues to support the malaria epidemic surveillance system to expand data collection and improvement to all health posts in the districts in Saint-Louis. Currently, there are 4 health posts reporting to the system in Saint-Louis and there are approximately 10-15 posts per district. To support reactive case detection, all health posts need to be reporting to the system, requiring increased number of supervision visits and improved transmission of data through an SMS platform. In 2015, the NMCP plans to continue expanding surveillance sites to cover all districts in Saint-Louis and covering two additional regions in the North (Louga and Matam Region). Weekly reporting will be introduced as standard procedure to these sites and eventually all health posts.

The data strike affecting the routine malaria data was lifted in March 2013 and the effort to backfill the database is complete as of 2014. With funding from the Global Fund and West Africa for Health and technical assistance provided by Oslo University, the DHIS2 was established by the MoH for their nationwide integrated health information system. The system design and training of district level data managers was completed in early 2015. There are planned quarterly reviews of the data collected through the DHIS2. Currently, the DHIS2 is reporting at 70% completeness for malaria indicators and the NMCP is continuing to collect information through Excel workbooks. At the request of the NMCP, PMI supported the update of a database developed in collaboration with RBM, based on EpiInfo^{TM} (DOS), known as the Roll Back Malaria Monitoring and Evaluation database software. The database was updated from the DOS-based version of EpiInfo™ (which was no longer supported by computers), to the new module of EpiInfo™ 7. With the development of the DHIS2, roll-out of this database is being reconsidered.

The cDHS has completed Phase 2 of data collection and the final report was disseminated in March 2015. Two hundred clusters for the DHS, and a random sample of approximately 20% of health facilities for the SPA, were included. Key findings from Phase 1 and 2 of data collection are reported in Table 1. The recent SPA results show that 94% of health facilities that offer malaria services had RDTs available and 80% had ACTs available. Senegal is the first PMI focus country to implement a cDHS which has helped strengthen capacity for data collection and use as well as informing malaria-specific programs. The cDHS is expected to be a permanent part of the MoH's data stream and the expectation is that fewer national household surveys will be needed.

Table 10. Monitoring and Evaluation Data Sources

Data Source	Survey Activities	Year								
		'10	'11	'12	'13	'14	'15	'16	'17	'18
National-level Household Surveys	Demographic Health Survey (DHS) and cDHS	X		X	X	X	X	(X)	(X)	(X)
	Universal coverage evaluation				X					
Health Facility Surveys	SPA survey as part of cDHS			X	X	X	X	(X)	(X)	(X)
Malaria Surveillance and Routine System Support	Malaria epidemic surveillance	X*	X*	X	X	X	X	(X)	(X)	(X)
	Case investigation			X*	X*	X	X	(X)	(X)	(X)
	SMC M&E					X	X	(X)	(X)	(X)
	Drug quality monitoring	X	X	X	X	X	X	(X)	(X)	(X)
	Routine data from health system through RBM database*	X*	X*	X*	X*	X*	X*	(X*)	(X*)	(X*)
	DHIS2 Integrated Routine Information System					X*	X*	(X*)	(X*)	(X*)
Therapeutic Efficacy monitoring	Therapeutic efficacy testing	X		X	X	X	X	(X)	(X)	(X)
Entomology	Entomological surveillance and resistance monitoring	X	X	X	X	X	X	(X)	(X)	(X)
	LLIN durability monitoring						X	(X)	(X)	(X)
Other malaria-related evaluations	Impact Evaluation				X			(X)		
* = Not PMI-funded (X) = Planned activity										

Plans and justification

Using FY 2016 funds, PMI plans to continue support for the expansion of case investigation in districts within the regions of Saint-Louis, Louga, and Matam that are classified as low transmission by the NMCP, with less than five cases per 1,000 population, as determined by the routine information system that includes the number of confirmed malaria cases identified at the community and facility level. Information on positive malaria cases will be sent to the district health supervisor and, within three days of notification, a team will be deployed to the community level to conduct a detailed investigation of the index case and screening of the five neighboring households, only testing individuals who are: 1) symptomatic, 2) have traveled recently, or 3) do not sleep under an ITN. Activities will be expanded into Saint-Louis District, completing the coverage of Saint-Louis Region and expanding into Louga Region and one to two districts of Matam Region. Support from PMI will contribute to key data collection and analysis activities, as well as enhancing activities to support pre-elimination objectives.

In accordance with WHOPES guidelines and recommendations, PMI will continue durability monitoring of LLINs distributed during the 2014 mass campaigns to estimate survivorship/attrition and physical integrity. With the planned campaign in 2016, PMI plans to conduct baseline and six-month follow-up laboratory testing on a sample of nets to ensure they adhere to WHOPES specifications for insecticide content.

Proposed activities with FY 2016 funding ($1,570,000)

1. *Technical assistance and operational support for a full malaria module, including biomarkers, as part of the continuous DHS (cDHS) ($450,000)*
With FY 2016 funding, PMI plans to maintain its support for the cDHS which is co-funded with other donors. The support includes technical assistance to the National Statistics and Demography Agency to continue strengthening their capacity to analyze and present the collected data.

2. *Strengthening and expanding epidemiologic malaria surveillance ($400,000)*
As Senegal moves toward pre-elimination and expands reactive case detection in the northern regions, PMI will continue to support the malaria surveillance system, including weekly case notification, in both the formal public health sector (hospitals, centers, and posts) and at the community level (health huts and DSDOMs). This system includes electronic transmission of data by short message service (SMS) and will be integrated with the DHIS2. This support will expand the system by recruiting new sites in all districts in Saint-Louis Region as well as districts in Louga and Matam regions.

3. *Case investigation in districts with incidence <5 per 1,000 ($400,000)*
As case detection is expanded in the northern districts with incidence <5 per 1,000, there will be training for additional CHWs, health post nurses, and district health supervisors for investigation of index cases and neighboring households. Weekly electronic data transmission through SMS will be supported. Results will be collected, analyzed, and shared by the NMCP through weekly bulletins.

4. *Monitoring and evaluation of seasonal malaria chemoprevention ($150,000)*
The NMCP will continue SMC in the four high transmission regions of southeastern Senegal: Tambacounda, Kédougou, Kolda, and Sédhiou. In accordance with the WHO field manual for SMC M&E, PMI will continue support for the existing routine health information system to monitor indicators relevant to SMC. PMI will support process monitoring and an end of season coverage survey. Molecular markers will be monitored.

5. *Monitoring and evaluation course by NMCP ($150,000)*
As part of the mid-term review of the strategic plan, the importance of M&E training at the regional and district level was recommended. PMI will support the NMCP in developing an updated M&E course that includes aspects of surveillance and monitoring related to pre-

elimination and elimination of malaria. This training workshop will then be rolled out to the regional and district levels to build and strengthen the M&E capacity of personnel nationally. The course that is planned to be developed will be malaria specific with the inclusion of pre-elimination and elimination M&E issues—specifically including lessons learned from activities currently being implemented in northern Senegal. M/Evaluation offers a regional malaria M&E course that will be used as the foundation for the Senegal-specific course. The course will be rolled out to all regions and districts in Senegal. The NMCP feels that in order to support pre-elimination activities that are being expanded in Senegal, there needs to be a strong cadre of M&E specialists at all levels to better collect, use, and manage information at lower levels.

6. *Two technical assistance visits from CDC ($20,000)*
CDC staff will provide technical support for M&E activities, including the expansion of the surveillance and routine malaria systems and providing input to the aspects of surveillance for the development of the M&E course in collaboration with M/Evaluation. Two visits are planned to provide follow-up of planned activities.

7. *LLIN durability monitoring*
Please see the proposed activities in the ITN section for budget and further details.

8. Operational research

NMCP Objectives
The goal of operational research in Senegal (which is grouped with M&E in the National Strategic Framework) is to provide data for decision making, in particular to evaluate issues related to achieving pre-elimination, both in the low transmission North and the high transmission South.

Progress since PMI was launched
Many partners are involved in conducting operational research in Senegal. PMI's support for OR has been complementary to those existing efforts. For example, MACEPA and UCAD are conducting studies of case investigation, MDA, MSAT, etc. in the North, while PMI has supported a study on the burden of malaria in nomadic pastoralists that move between the North and South. In the South, the evaluation of SMC implemented by UCAD is being co-funded by PMI and Wellcome Trust. PMI also funded a study to evaluate causes of persistent high transmission in a district (Vélingara) in which all interventions had been scaled up, and to suggest strategies to address the challenges identified. Furthermore, PMI funding supported the operational research study on PECADOM Plus conducted by the NMCP and Peace Corps. Please see the table and descriptions below for a summary of all PMI-funded operational studies to date.

Table 11. PMI-funded Operational Research Studies

Completed OR Studies			
Title	**Start date**	**End date**	**Budget**
Evaluation of the diagnostic algorithm	9/2012	6/2014	$125,000
Burden of malaria among nomadic pastoralists	8/2014	10/2014	$100,000
Qualitative study of seasonal malaria chemoprevention	9/2014	3/2015	$50,000
Qualitative study of causes of elevated transmission in Vélingara	11/2014	3/2015	$40,000

Planned OR Studies FY 2016			
Title	**Start date (est.)**	**End date (est.)**	**Budget**
Collection of dried blood spot samples and PCR Analysis for Parasitemia Prevalence in Low Transmission Setting	10/2016	10/2017	$50,000

Evaluation of the diagnostic algorithm. A study of the effectiveness of the diagnostic algorithm for identifying patients with fever or history of fever that have malaria parasitemia was completed in early 2014, and found that application of the algorithm results in an unacceptable number of missed cases, particularly in areas of high transmission. Based on these results, the NMCP has changed diagnostic policy, and is transitioning to testing of all patients with fever or a history of fever by 2017.

Burden of malaria among nomadic pastoralists. In late 2014, a study on the burden of malaria among nomadic pastoralists found that though parasite prevalence is far lower than expected (lower than 1%), nomadic pastoralists have sub-optimal access to mass distributions of LLINs, access to care, and messaging regarding malaria. Interventions are being designed to reach this group, including introduction of nomadic home-based care providers.

Qualitative study of seasonal malaria chemoprevention. Results are pending for a study on the acceptability of SMC.

Qualitative study of causes of elevated transmission in Vélingara. A qualitative study to explore reasons for ongoing high transmission in a district in which all interventions, including IRS, have been scaled up found that while people value and use their LLINs, many participate in late-night discussions over tea until well after midnight, and many others sleep outside to guard crops or belongings, and nets may or may not be used. In addition, there were many barriers to care seeking identified as well as frequent stockouts of malaria diagnostics and treatment. This study contributed to the data that led to the decision to stop IRS in that district, and to focus on improving the supply chain, reinforcing routine LLIN distribution and messages to use LLINs outdoors, and community case management, including PECADOM Plus.

Plans and Justification

Given the low national prevalence of malaria (1.2%) reported in the latest 2014 cDHS with reported malaria incidence in the northern regions at <5 per 1,000, the NMCP is requesting support to add molecular diagnostics to samples collected from children under five during the continuous DHS to determine the proportion of sub-microscopic asymptomatic parasite reservoir among children by transmission zone and to examine parasite diversity and movement. As Senegal moves towards pre-elimination in the northern districts, collecting this information would assist the NMCP to determine what is missed by RDTs and slides and evaluate the issues related to achieving pre-elimination. At the same time hemoglobin and RDTs/slides are collected from children under five in the cDHS, filter paper would be collected that would make possible both PCR and serologic analysis.

Proposed activities with FY 2016 funding ($50,000)

1. Inclusion of dried blood spot samples in the cDHS for PCR analysis and/or serology ($50,000)

This budget will cover the laboratory work for the collected samples. It is anticipated that the UCAD Parasitology laboratory, which already does the blood slide reading, would also do the molecular work.

At the time of developing this operational plan, the inter-agency Pre-Elimination Working Group and Monitoring and Evaluation Team are planning to discuss the use of PCR analysis and serology to develop updated guidance for PMI. Currently, any collection of dried blood spot samples for PCR analysis and/or serology is considered an OR activity by PMI.

9. Staffing and administration

Two health professionals serve as resident advisors to oversee PMI in Senegal, one representing CDC and one representing USAID. In addition, one or more Foreign Service Nationals (FSNs) work as part of the PMI team. All PMI staff members are part of a single interagency team led by the USAID Mission Director or his/her designee in country. The PMI team shares responsibility for development and implementation of PMI strategies and work plans, coordination with national authorities, managing collaborating agencies and supervising day-to-day activities. Candidates for resident advisor positions (whether initial hires or replacements) will be evaluated and/or interviewed jointly by USAID and CDC, and both agencies will be involved in hiring decisions, with the final decision made by the individual agency.

The PMI professional staff work together to oversee all technical and administrative aspects of the PMI, including finalizing details of the project design, implementing malaria prevention and treatment activities, monitoring and evaluation of outcomes and impact, reporting of results, and providing guidance to PMI partners.

The PMI lead in country is the USAID Mission Director. The day-to-day lead for PMI is delegated to the USAID Health Office Director and thus the two PMI resident advisors, one from USAID and one from CDC, report to the USAID Health Office Director for day-to-day leadership, and work together as a part of a single interagency team. The technical expertise housed in Atlanta and Washington guides PMI programmatic efforts.

The two PMI resident advisors are based within the USAID health office and are expected to spend approximately half their time sitting with and providing technical assistance to the national malaria control programs and partners.

Locally-hired staff to support PMI activities either in Ministries or in USAID will be approved by the USAID Mission Director. Because of the need to adhere to specific country policies and USAID accounting regulations, any transfer of PMI funds directly to Ministries or host governments will need to be approved by the USAID Mission Director and Controller, in addition to the US Global Malaria Coordinator.

Proposed activities with FY 2016 funding ($1,512,000)

These funds are slated to be used for coordination and management of all in-country PMI activities including support for salaries and benefits for two resident advisors and local staff, office equipment and supplies, and routine administration and coordination expenses.

1. *USAID technical staff ($928,035)*
   Funding will support the salaries for one USAID resident advisor and local staff.

2. *CDC technical staff ($583,965)*
   Funding will support the salary and expenses for one CDC resident advisor.

Table 1: Budget Breakdown by Mechanism

President's Malaria Initiative – Senegal

Planned Malaria Obligations for FY 2016

Mechanism	Geographic Area	Activity	Budget ($)	%
CDC IAA	Nationwide	In-country staff & administration, technical assistance for entomological monitoring and surveillance	$647,965	3
GEMS II	IRS areas	Environmental compliance	$30,000	<1
HDS-Africa	Nationwide	LLIN durability monitoring	$111,000	<1
IRS 2 TO6	Targeted districts	IRS operations	$2,470,000	11
Measure DHS	Nationwide	Continuous DHS, including PCR/serology analysis of dried blood spots	$500,000	2
National Drug Control Laboratory	9 sites	Drug quality monitoring	$200,000	<1
National Malaria Control Program	Nationwide	Strengthen microscopic diagnosis of malaria ; intensification of integrated home-based management of malaria and expansion of PECADOM Plus; implementation of SMC; expansion of pre-referral treatment and use of primaquine; program supervision; support for NMCP staff attendance at scientific/technical meetings; community sensitization for IRS and SMC; surveillance; case investigation.	$5,070,000	23

TBD	Nationwide	Operational costs of maintaining routine ITN distribution system; strengthening malaria in pregnancy services; support for case management activities at the facility and community level; community mobilization and implementation of BCC activities; strengthening supply chain management; performance-based financing.	$4,450,000	20
TBD-Supply Chain Contract	Nationwide	Procurement of LLINs, ACTs, RDTs, SP-AQ, primaquine, rectal & injectable artesunate, and laboratory consumables.	$7,018,000	32
UCAD-Entomology	Targeted districts	Entomological monitoring	$400,000	2
UCAD-Parasitology	Nationwide	Therapeutic efficacy testing and quality control for malaria diagnostics	$125,000	<1
US Peace Corps	Nationwide	Support to Peace Corps malaria activities	$25,000	<1
US Pharmacopeia	Nationwide	Technical assistance for drug quality monitoring	$25,000	<1
USAID	Nationwide	In-country staff & administration	$928,035	4
Total			$22,000,000	100

Table 2: Budget Breakdown by Activity

President's Malaria Initiative – Senegal

Planned Malaria Obligations for FY 2016

Proposed Activity	Mechanism	Budget		Geographic Area	Description
		Total $	Commodity $		
PREVENTIVE ACTIVITIES					
Insecticide-treated Nets					
Procurement of ITNs	TBD - Supply Chain Contract	4,000,000	4,000,000	Nationwide	1,200,000 LLINs to support routine channels.
Operational costs of maintaining routine distribution system	TBD	700,000		Nationwide	Transport, support materials, supervision.
LLIN durability monitoring	HDS-Africa	111,000		Nationwide	Support for training and field data collection, supplies and equipment for cone bioassays
SUBTOTAL ITNs		**4,811,000**	4,000,000		
Indoor Residual Spraying					
Indoor residual spraying operations	IRS 2 TO6	2,470,000		Hot spots in eligible districts	Technical assistance and purchase of insecticides.

65

Activity	Source			Location	Description
Strengthen entomologic capabilities and entomologic monitoring	UCAD - Entomology	400,000		Nationwide	Entomological monitoring (20 sites).
	CDC IAA	44,000	15,000	N/A	Technical assistance for entomologic monitoring ($29,000 TA, $15,000 supplies).
Environmental compliance	GEMS II	30,000		IRS areas	One visit to conduct required environmental compliance inspection.
SUBTOTAL IRS		**2,944,000**	15,000		
Malaria in Pregnancy					
Reinforce provision of effective malaria in pregnancy services in health facilities and through outreach strategies	TBD	700,000		Nationwide	Monitoring and supportive supervision, update materials to reflect revised guidelines, training of new staff. Cups and water filters as needed for directly-observed treatment with SP.
SUBTOTAL MIP		700,000	0		
SUBTOTAL PREVENTIVE		**8,455,000**	4,015,000		
CASE MANAGEMENT					
Diagnosis and Treatment					
Strengthen microscopic diagnosis of malaria	NMCP	200,000		Nationwide	Training, supervision, quality assurance, and quality control for microscopy.
Procurement of microscopes and laboratory consumables	TED - Supply Chain Contract	30,000	30,000	Nationwide	Laboratory consumables and replacement of aging microscopes, as needed.
Procurement of RDTs	TBD - Supply Chain Contract	1,500,000	1,500,000	Nationwide	2,500,000 RDTs

Activity	Implementer			Location	Description
Quality control of microscopy and RDTs	UCAD - Parasitology	25,000		Nationwide	Support for the implementation of quality control programs for both microscopy and RDTs, in conjunction with NMCP and the Université Cheikh Anta Diop.
Improve case management at health facilities	TBD	500,000		Nationwide	Support for training and supervision of malaria case management at all levels of the health system, including the private sector.
Strengthen community case management	TBD	500,000		Nationwide	Support for community case management of malaria by CHWs in 1,620 functional health huts. Includes training, supervision, and monitoring of staff.
Intensification of integrated home-based management of malaria (PECADOM) and operational costs for expansion of PECADOM Plus	NMCP	1,500,000		Selected Districts	Support for the new recruitment, training, and supervision of DSDOMs to provide malaria diagnosis and treatment as part of an integrated package of services. Extension of PECADOM Plus to up to 40 districts.
Procurement of ACTs	TBD - Supply Chain Contract	783,000	783,000	Nationwide	Approximately 800,000 ACTs.
Operational costs for SMC implementation	NMCP	1,500,000		Kédougou, Sédhiou, Kolda, Tambacounda	Operational costs of the SMC campaign in 4 districts for 3-4 months
Procurement of drugs for SMC implementation	TBD-Supply Chain Contract	600,000	600,000	Kédougou, Sédhiou, Kolda, Tambacounda	Monthly doses of SP-AQ for approximately 600,000 children (ages 3 months to 10 years), administered by community volunteers for 3-4 months during the

Activity	Responsible Party			Location	Description
					high transmission season.
Operational costs of expanding pre-referral treatment to the community level	NMCP	150,000		Nationwide	Support for progressive nationwide scale-up of community-level pre-referral treatment, adding another 10 high transmission districts.
Procurement of rectal artesunate for pre-referral treatment	TBD - Supply Chain Contract	40,000	40,000	Nationwide	Approximately 45,000 doses (100mg per dose) to provide for community level expansion.
Procurement of injectable artesunate for treatment of severe malaria	TBD - Supply Chain Contract	55,000	55,000	Nationwide	Approximately 21,000 treatments (5 ampules per treatment) of injectable artesunate to treat severe malaria cases referred to the hospital or health center level (estimate is for approx. 30% of need based on 2013 severe malaria incidence levels).
Procurement of primaquine	TBD - Supply Chain Contract	10,000	10,000	Pre-elimination districts	Procurement costs include primaquine for single low-dose treatment.
Expansion of low-dose primaquine administration in elimination districts	NMCP	40,000		Pre-elimination districts	Support for introduction of single low-dose treatment in one pre-elimination region.
Therapeutic efficacy monitoring	UCAD-Parasitology	100,000		2 sites	Therapeutic efficacy studies in 4 sites (2 sites per year on a rotating basis).
Subtotal Diagnosis and Treatment		**7,533,000**	3,018,000		
Pharmaceutical Management					
Supply chain management and drug management	TBD	800,000		Nationwide	Support for the NMCP to improve quantification through regular consumption data collection from the

	Partner				
from central to peripheral level					peripheral level.
Drug quality monitoring and advocacy	National Drug Control Laboratory	200,000		9 sites	Sampling and testing antimalarials from 9 sites nationwide.
	USP	25,000		Nationwide	Technical assistance for accreditation and drug quality monitoring.
Subtotal Pharmaceutical Management		**1,025,000**	0		
SUBTOTAL CASE MANAGEMENT		**8,558,000**	3,018,000		
HEALTH SYSTEM STRENGTHENING / CAPACITY BUILDING					
Support to NMCP to enable program supervision	NMCP	250,000		Nationwide	Support visits by national staff to regional and district levels.
State of the art capacity building opportunities	NMCP	30,000		N/A	Support participation in international technical scientific and professional meetings that present NMCP staff opportunities to learn best practices, share experiences, and develop networks. Potential meetings will include the American Society for Tropical Medicine and Hygiene and Pan-African Malaria Conference. ASTMH, MIM. 2 trips, 2 people each.
Malariology course	NMCP	100,000			The NMCP is requesting PMI's support for the creation of a malariology course (including curriculum development) that would be offered to health staff at various levels and would allow for in-country training opportunities.

Activity	Partner	Amount	Location	Description
Support to Peace Corps malaria-related activities	Small Projects Assistance Peace Corps	25,000	Peace Corps Volunteer Communities	Support for specific malaria-related Peace Corps volunteer projects.
Support for Performance-Based Financing for malaria indicators	TBD	150,000	Targeted districts	Continued support for the collection of malaria indicators under the Performance-Based Financing model.
Improve governance of local health committees	TBD	200,000	Nationwide	Support for the local government to include malaria and other health priorities in their local development plans and increase participation of communities in decision-making regarding health issues.
SUBTOTAL HSS & CAPACITY BUILDING		**755,000**	0	
BEHAVIOR CHANGE COMMUNICATION				
Development, implementation, and evaluation of BCC activities	TBD	800,000	Nationwide	Overall support for the development, production, and dissemination of IEC/BCC materials, including support for the national IEC/BCC Committee to ensure harmonization of messages among partners.
Community sensitization and mobilization for IRS	NMCP	100,000	Hot spots in eligible districts	Implementation of radio spots, community meetings, and house-to-house visits to ensure high community acceptance of IRS in spray areas.
Community sensitization and mobilization for SMC	NMCP	100,000	Kédougou, Sédhiou, Kolda, Tambacounda	Promotion of SMC through radio spots, community meetings, and house-to-house visits in regions targeted for this intervention.

Activity	Implementer	Amount		Location	Description
Promotion of LLIN use	TBD	100,000		Nationwide	Social marketing of LLINs in the private sector, including packaging and transportation to wholesalers.
SUBTOTAL BCC		**1,100,000**	0		
MONITORING AND EVALUATION					
Support to the malaria module in cDHS	Measure DHS	450,000		Nationwide	Technical assistance for sampling and analysis ($100,000). Operational support ($350,000) for a full malaria module as part of cDHS, including biomarkers. Co-funding from other donors.
Strengthening malaria surveillance and response	NMCP	400,000		Nationwide	Strengthening notification, particularly using mobile communication. ($75,000 of funds reserved for potential response to epidemics).
Case investigation in districts with incidence <5 per 1,000	NMCP	400,000		Pre-elimination districts	Support training for the investigation of index cases and neighboring households and weekly electronic data transmission with DHIS2 integration.
Monitoring and evaluation of seasonal malaria chemoprevention	NMCP	150,000		Kédougou, Sédhiou, Kolda, Tambacounda	Support process monitoring, end of season coverage survey and molecular markers.
Monitoring and evaluation course by NMCP	NMCP	150,000		Nationwide	Support to the NMCP for the development of an updated M&E course that includes aspects of surveillance and monitoring related to pre-elimination and elimination of malaria.

Technical assistance in M&E from CDC	CDC IAA	20,000	Nationwide	CDC will provide technical support for M&E activities, including the expansion of the surveillance and routine malaria systems and assist with surveillance aspects of the M&E course in collaboration with M/Evaluation.
SUBTOTAL M&E		**1,570,000**	0	
OPERATIONS RESEARCH				
Inclusion of dried blood spot samples in the cDHS for PCR analysis and/or serology	Measure DHS	50,000	Nationwide	Collection of dried blood spot samples in the cDHS for PCR analysis and/or serology to capture sub-microscopic infections for more accurate tracking of malaria parasite prevalence as the country moves towards pre-elimination.
SUBTOTAL OR		**50,000**	0	
IN-COUNTRY STAFFING AND ADMINISTRATION				
USAID Technical Staff	USAID	928,035		Support the salaries and expenses for one USAID resident advisor and local staff.
CDC Technical Staff	CDC	583,965		Support the salary and expenses for one CDC resident advisor.
SUBTOTAL IN-COUNTRY STAFFING		**1,512,000**	0	
GRAND TOTAL		**22,000,000**	7,033,000